EP Language Arts 4
Workbook

This book belongs to:

_____

EP Language Arts 4 Workbook

ISBN-13: 978-1974593880
ISBN-10: 1974593886

First Edition: September 2017

About this Workbook

This is an offline workbook for Easy Peasy All-in-One Homeschool's Language Arts 4 course. We've modified and expanded upon the online activities and printable worksheets available at the Easy Peasy All-in-One Homeschool website (www.allinonehomeschool.com) so that your child can work offline if desired. Whether you use the online or offline versions, or a combination of both, your child will enjoy these supplements to the Easy Peasy Language Arts course.

How to use this Workbook

This workbook is designed to be used in conjunction with Easy Peasy's Language Arts 4 Parent's Guide. As you proceed through the Parent's Guide, use this workbook to exercise your child's language arts skills.

This workbook follows the EP online Language Arts course in sequential order, providing 180 daily activity worksheets which can replace online activities and printable worksheets. The daily worksheets are designed with the following guidelines in mind:

- ## To supplement daily lessons
  This workbook on its own supplements, but does not replace, EP's daily lessons. Be sure to check the daily lesson on the website or in the Parent's Guide before having your child do the workbook activities.

- ## To serve as an alternative to online activities
  This workbook serves as an alternative to the activities posted online, providing offline activities in sufficient quantities and varieties to challenge your child. When used in conjunction with the Parent's Guide, this workbook becomes a complete offline course.

Please note, in the various places where nouns, verbs, and adjectives are practiced, certain words can be categorized in more than one place (you can go for a swim [noun] or you can swim [verb]). If your child marks one of them differently than the answer key indicates, have a conversation with them to find out why.

A full answer key for this workbook can be found in the back of the Language Arts 4 Parent's Guide. Answers are *not* included in this workbook.

Completion Chart for Lessons 1 - 45

#	Lesson	#	Lesson	#	Lesson
1	speaking	16	spelling	31	writing/nouns/verbs
2	syllables	17	writing	32	writing/sentence types
3	spelling	18	spelling	33	main idea
4	rhyming words	19	action/linking verbs	34	main idea
5	poetry writing	20	writing	35	writing
6	spelling	21	spelling	36	writing/main idea
7	limerick writing	22	writing	37	writing
8	spelling	23	spelling	38	spelling
9	nouns	24	nouns/verbs	39	reading comprehension
10	limerick writing	25	writing	40	writing
11	alphabetical order	26	sentence types	41	writing/verbs
12	limerick writing	27	writing	42	writing
13	common/proper nouns	28	writing	43	spelling
14	action verbs	29	common/proper nouns	44	quotation marks
15	writing	30	writing	45	comic

Completion Chart for Lessons 46 - 90

46	writing	61	writing	76	adjectives
47	writing	62	writing	77	writing
48	writing	63	writing	78	writing
49	quotation marks	64	writing	79	adjectives
50	writing	65	writing	80	speaking
51	writing	66	writing	81	writing
52	writing	67	writing	82	writing
53	writing	68	writing	83	writing
54	quotation marks	69	writing	84	parts of speech
55	writing	70	writing	85	writing
56	writing/proper nouns	71	writing	86	writing
57	writing	72	editing	87	feedback
58	writing/linking verbs	73	feedback	88	spelling
59	nouns/verbs/idioms	74	adjectives	89	writing/punctuation
60	writing	75	formal letter	90	writing

Completion Chart for Lessons 91-135

91	writing	106	parts of speech	121	book review
92	writing	107	adverbs/spelling	122	book review
93	homophones	108	editing/autobiography	123	parts of speech/autobiography
94	writing	109	good vs. well	124	editing/autobiography
95	writing	110	writing	125	biography
96	spelling	111	writing/autobiography	126	biography
97	spelling	112	spelling/autobiography	127	biography
98	nouns	113	semicolons/autobiography	128	biography
99	idioms	114	writing	129	biography
100	spelling	115	paragraphs/writing/autobiography	130	grammar review
101	copywork	116	spelling/adverbs	131	biography
102	writing	117	editing/autobiography	132	editing
103	writing	118	spelling	133	capitalization/spelling
104	writing	119	adjectives/autobiography	134	writing
105	writing	120	parts of speech	135	writing

Completion Chart for Lessons 136-180

136	writing	151	parts of speech	166	editing
137	editing	152	vowel sounds/ adverbs	167	final project
138	writing/adverbs	153	nouns	168	final project
139	adverbs	154	writing	169	final project
140	writing/adverbs	155	spelling	170	final project
141	main idea	156	correct the sentences	171	final project
142	inferences	157	homophones/ homonyms	172	final project
143	writing/inferences	158	writing	173	final project
144	linking verbs	159	friendly letter	174	final project
145	verbs	160	acrostic poem	175	final project
146	verbs	161	descriptive writing	176	final project
147	verbs/adverbs	162	descriptive writing	177	final project
148	writing	163	descriptive writing	178	final project
149	grammar	164	descriptive writing	179	final project
150	verbs/adverbs	165	editing	180	final project

Speaking

Recite the poem excerpt below. First read the stanzas out loud to yourself for practice, getting a feel for the rhyme and rhythm of the poem. Then read them aloud to an audience. Be sure to speak loudly and clearly. (NOTE: the teaching lesson for this and every worksheet is located in the Parent's Guide. That separate book is necessary to make the course complete.)

The Shepherd Boy - Emily S. Oakey

Little Roy led his sheep down to pasture,
And his cows, by the side of the brook;
But his cows never drank any water,
And his sheep never needed a crook.

For the pasture was gay as a garden,
And it glowed with a flowery red;
But the meadows had never a grass blade,
And the brooklet—it slept in its bed:

And it lay without sparkle or murmur,
Nor reflected the blue of the skies;
But the music was made by the shepherd,
And the sparkle was all in his eyes.

Oh, he sang like a bird in the summer!
And, if sometimes you fancied a bleat,
That, too, was the voice of the shepherd,
And not of the lambs at his feet.

And the glossy brown cows were so gentle
That they moved at the touch of his hand
O'er the wonderful, rosy-red meadow,
And they stood at the word of command.

So he led all his sheep to the pasture,
And his cows, by the side of the brook;
Though it rained, yet the rain never pattered
O'er the beautiful way that they took.

Syllables

How many syllables are in the following words? Write the number of syllables in the blank beside the word. If you need help, put your hand under your chin and say the word out loud. The number of times your hand goes down is the number of syllables in the word.

carrot _____   aquarium _____

burger _____   Philadelphia _____

basketball _____   capitalization _____

umbrella _____   electrifying _____

butterfly _____   encyclopedia _____

airplane _____   Mesopotamia _____

caterpillar _____   mysterious _____

giraffe _____   cantaloupe _____

bottle _____   experience _____

telephone _____   aluminum _____

Guess the Word

Use the blanks below to guess the words. The words are in the Parent's Guide. You can use the alphabet above each set of blanks to keep track of the letters you've guessed by crossing them out. Can you guess each word before you get 10 missed letters?

A B C D E F G H I J K L M N O P Q R S T U V W X Y Z

_ _ _ _ _ _ _ _ _ _ _

A B C D E F G H I J K L M N O P Q R S T U V W X Y Z

_ _ _ _ _ _ _ _ _ _ _

A B C D E F G H I J K L M N O P Q R S T U V W X Y Z

_ _ _ _ _ _ _ _ _ _ _

A B C D E F G H I J K L M N O P Q R S T U V W X Y Z

_ _ _ _ _ _ _ _ _ _ _

A B C D E F G H I J K L M N O P Q R S T U V W X Y Z

_ _ _ _ _ _ _ _ _ _ _

Writing

Write a list of ten pairs of rhyming words, five of which have to be at least two syllables long. If you need help getting started, here are a few words for which you could find rhymes: *darker*, *rounded*, *lighten*.

_____ _____

_____ _____

_____ _____

_____ _____

_____ _____

Poetry Writing

Write an ABAB poem. Your poem should be four lines where lines one and three rhyme and lines two and four rhyme. Each line should have 7 or 8 syllables. You can use some of the rhyming words you wrote in lesson 4 to help you get started.

_____

_____

_____

_____

_____

_____

_____

Spelling Bee

Fill in the missing words from the story. The list of words is in the Parent's Guide.
Spell each word the best that you can and learn from any mistakes that you make.

We had a wonderful family _____ to

the _____. First, we built sandcastles

using our _____ and _____.

Next, we went on a hunt for sea _____.

My favorite was the _____ sea anemone I

found in the shallow tide pool. Finally, we went

_____ in the _____.

We practically _____ in all of that salt!

Limerick Writing

Write a limerick. Limericks are fun poems in the form AABBA. The A lines are longer and the B lines are shorter. If you clapped the rhythm, you would clap three times for the A lines and twice for the B lines. Here is an example:

I once spent a day at the zoo.
My sister and brother did, too.
We saw a big bear,
An ape and a hare
And a peacock a deep shade of blue.

_____

_____

_____

_____

_____

Word Builder

How many words can you make from the letters in the box below? Only use letters that are adjacent to each other (see the example).

B	R	A	S	B	L	A	K
N	I	S	H	E	U	C	Y
O	S	H	G	D	J	K	S
K	B	G	I	L	C	N	P
L	M	Q	U	S	W	Y	A
I	N	O	E	P	T	K	S
O	L	E	S	R	D	B	T
F	L	H	T	C	F	H	M
C	E	D	U	E	W	T	A
A	R	G	L	L	Z	Y	T
N	L	H	S	M	A	E	E
B	W	A	Y	R	G	F	D
E	D	O	T	U	K	T	E
P	R	L	C	N	D	G	F

____ brains ____   _____

_____   _____

_____   _____

_____   _____

_____   _____

_____   _____

Noun Review

Remember that a noun is a person, place, thing, or idea. Color in the clouds below that contain nouns.

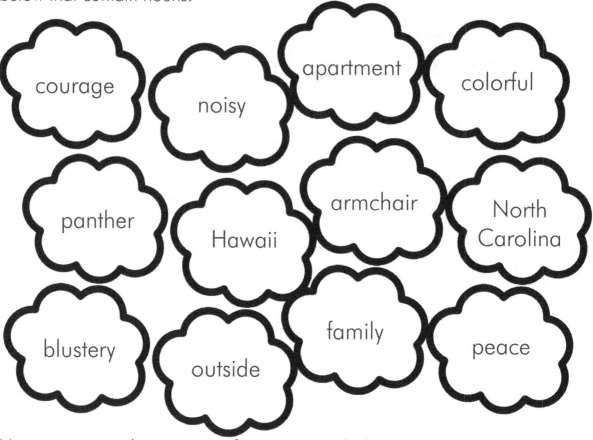

Now come up with ten nouns of your own. Include a common noun, a proper noun, a concrete noun, an abstract noun, a compound noun, and a collective noun.

_____   _____

_____   _____

_____   _____

_____   _____

_____   _____

Limerick Writing

Write another limerick. Remember that limericks are fun poems in the form AABBA. If you need a refresher about limericks, see lesson 7.

How many lines are there in a limerick? _____

Which lines rhyme in a limerick? _____

_____

Here is another example of a limerick:

There was an old lady named Jane
Who took a walk down the lane.
She soon turned around,
For quickly she found
She forgot to carry her cane.

_____

_____

_____

_____

Alphabetical Order

Put the words in each section in alphabetical order. Compare the first letter of each word and order the words based on the order of the alphabet. If the first letter is the same, compare the second letters of the words. If the second letter is the same, compare the third letters, and so on.

fly, flying, flip, flap, flamingo

_____   _____

_____   _____

crunch, crust, crutch, crush, crumble

_____   _____

_____   _____

ask, aspirin, ashes, ascend, as

_____   _____

_____   _____

blend, bleach, bless, blew, blender

_____   _____   _____

_____   _____

Limerick Writing

Write another limerick. Remember that limericks are fun poems in the form AABBA. If you need a refresher about limericks, see lesson 7.

How many lines are there in a limerick? _____

Which lines rhyme in a limerick? _____

_____

Here is another example of a limerick:

I was in bed sick yesterday.
I hadn't the strength left to play.
But when I awoke,
As soon as I spoke,
I realized I'm better today!

_____

_____

_____

_____

Common and Proper Nouns

As a reminder, a common noun is a general person, place, thing, or idea. A proper noun is a specific person, place, thing, or idea. Proper nouns are capitalized because they are names.

Underline the common nouns in these sentences.

Uncle Daniel works at the library.

Sandra makes the most delicious muffins.

There are four new pandas at Metro Zoo.

William, Nathaniel, and Braden won the game.

The burgers from Red Robin taste the best.

Underline the proper nouns in these sentences.

The largest planet is Jupiter.

The snow piled up in Minneapolis last year.

Anne of Green Gables is a great book.

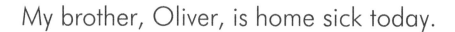

My brother, Oliver, is home sick today.

It's so hot in Florida.

Action Verbs

Remember that action verbs tell what someone or something does or is doing.
Taking each word as a verb, color in the flip flops below that contain action verbs.

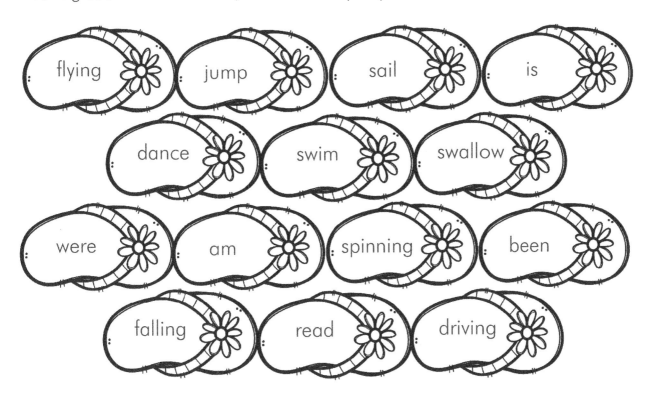

Now come up with ten action verbs of your own.

_____   _____

_____   _____

_____   _____

_____   _____

_____   _____

Writing

Read these first two stanzas of the poem *Speak Gently* by David Bates:

Speak gently; it is better far
To rule by love than fear:
Speak gently; let no harsh words mar
The good we might do here.

Speak gently to the little child;
Its love be sure to gain;
Teach it in accents soft and mild;
It may not long remain.

What form, or rhyme scheme, is the poem written in? _____

How many syllables are in each line? _____

Write a poem with two stanzas following the same format.

_____

_____

_____

_____

_____

_____

_____

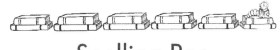

Spelling Bee

Fill in the missing words from the story. The list of words is in the Parent's Guide.
Spell each word the best that you can and learn from any mistakes that you make.

The Kentucky Derby has been _____ the

"most _____ two minutes in sports." This

title refers to the time it takes the _____

to complete their run around the track. Bigger than

most races, the Derby features _____

horses running like the wind around the track in an

attempt to win the two _____ dollar prize.

The Kentucky Derby takes place on the first

_____ in May and has since 1875. This

makes it the _____ continually held

sporting event in America.

Writing

Write a poem in any form you'd like. It doesn't even have to rhyme if you don't want it to. Can you make it more than one stanza? Can you use a new vocabulary word or two?

_____

_____

_____

_____

_____

_____

_____

_____

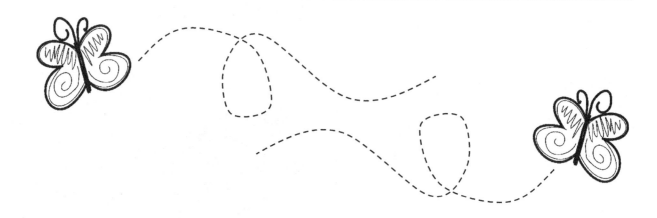

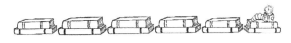

Spelling

Unscramble the following words. Can you rearrange the letters so that they make actual words? If you need help, look at the definition underneath each word.

UARYLOCBVA

_____

Words and their definitions.

TCRPEMOU

_____

A machine used for storing and processing data.

INECLP

_____

A writing utensil.

OBULTRE

_____

Difficulty; problems.

EONUINTC

_____

To keep going.

RENTSGTH

_____

Being strong.

EETLHM

_____

A hard, protective sort of hat.

RVEDSEE

_____

Be worthy of.

IQYULET

_____

Without making much noise.

Action and Linking Verbs

As a reminder, an action verb tells what someone or something does. A linking verb links a subject and predicate without showing action. Underline the verb in each sentence below. On the line beside it, describe the type of verb as either A for action or L for linking.

Her father is a veterinarian. _____

Briley delighted the crowd. _____

The dinner looks tasty. _____

The skaters are fast. _____

My mom paid for my dinner. _____

The boys tossed the football. _____

My writing assignment was long. _____

The girl sighed loudly. _____

We quickly became great friends. _____

Sarah used chopsticks easily. _____

Ezra seems lonely today. _____

The bus arrived later than expected. _____

Writing

Write a poem in any form you'd like. If you need help getting started, you could try using a repeating line. (This is just an idea to help if you're stuck, but you don't have to write your poem this way.) Here's an example of a repeating line poem:

It's morning now, time to start the day.
It's morning now, I think I will go play.

Spelling

Listen to your spelling words as they are read to you from the Parent's Guide. All of these words have the oo sound like in the word coop.

_____   _____

_____   _____

_____   _____

_____   _____

_____   _____

_____

Writing

Write about your first day stranded on an island.

_____

_____

_____

_____

_____

_____

_____

_____

Spelling

Fill in the blanks with the spelling words that best fit the sentence. All of these words have the OO sound.

I got an extra __ __ __ __ __ of ice cream.

We practiced our dance __ __ __ __ __ __ __ __ all day.

The roller coaster had a tall __ __ __ __.

The nurse bandaged my sister's __ __ __ __ __.

Daniel shot the ball straight into the __ __ __ __.

I bought a __ __ __ __ __ __ __ __ __ on our trip.

A __ __ __ __ __ __ __ got into our trash can.

My grandmother cooks delicious __ __ __ __.

The __ __ __ __ __ __ returned safely from deployment.

We had a __ __ __ __ __ at the craft fair.

I used the __ __ __ __ __ to clean the kitchen.

Writing

Write ten nouns on the lines below: five common and five proper. Be sure to include people, places, things, and ideas. Then write ten verbs: five action and five linking.

common	proper

☑ n
☑ o
☑ u
☐ n
☐ s

action	linking

☑ v
☑ e
☑ r
☐ b
☐ s

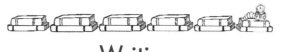

Writing

Write a how-to survival guide. Pick one survival skill: building a shelter, cooking dandelions, making a fire, anything you can think of that might be helpful. Write a how-to. Include an introduction sentence telling what you are going to teach. Then write in numbered steps what you need to do. Write every step (for example: 1. Look for dandelions that are already flowering.) Write as many steps as you can.

_____

_____

_____

_____

_____

_____

_____

_____

_____

Sentence Types

Read about the different kinds of sentences, and then write your own sentence of each type on the lines.

Declarative – a sentence that makes a statement.
Example: Pizza is my favorite food.

_____

Interrogative – a sentence that asks a question.
Example: What is your favorite food?

_____

Exclamatory – a sentence that shows strong feeling and ends with an exclamation mark.
Example: The dog stole my pizza!

_____

Imperative – a sentence that gives a command.
Example: Bring my pizza back right now.

_____

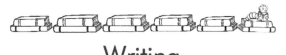

Writing

Write two declarative sentences, two interrogative sentences, two exclamatory sentences, and two imperative sentences. Can you make them all into a story?

_____

_____

_____

_____

_____

_____

_____

_____

_____

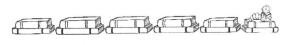

Writing

Write two declarative sentences, two interrogative sentences, two exclamatory sentences, and two imperative sentences. These should be new sentences! Can you make them all into a story?

_____

_____

_____

_____

_____

_____

_____

Common and Proper Nouns

Sort the words into the correct box.

Christmas	Monday	park	sandwich	girl	Disneyland
Nashville	rocket	Alaska	Earth	dog	bus

Proper Nouns

_____ _____

_____ _____

_____ _____

Common Nouns

_____ _____

_____ _____

_____ _____

Match the proper noun to its common noun by drawing a line between them.

Matthew	holiday
Easter	country
Friday	landmark
Mount Rushmore	boy
June	day
Canada	month

Writing

Write a short story about being alone (whether on an island, in the woods, at home, or wherever). Use at least one of each type of sentence. See lesson 26 if you need a reminder about the different sentence types.

_____

_____

_____

_____

_____

_____

_____

_____

Handwriting

Write the longest sentence you can find in a book you are reading. Use your very best handwriting and be sure to correctly copy all of the spelling, punctuation, and capitalization.

_____

_____

_____

_____

Nouns and Verbs

Underline the proper noun:

My best friend, Patricia, is a gymnast.

Underline the common noun:

The boy was crying when he got hurt.

Underline the linking verb:

You look tired today.

Underline the action verb (pay attention!):

Brooke went to dance class yesterday.

Handwriting

Copy each type of sentence from a book you are reading: a declarative sentence, an interrogatory sentence, an exclamatory sentence, and an imperative sentence. Write carefully and neatly.

Declarative:

_____

_____

Interrogatory:

_____

_____

Exclamatory:

_____

_____

Imperative:

_____

_____

Main Idea

Draw a line from the bee to the flower that contains the main idea of each set.

She needs to eat more.

Our cat is a really skinny cat.

The vet said to give her more treats.

It has rained for days.

The creek is flooding.

We've been stuck inside.

The phone wakes me up.

The phone makes me jump.

Our phone is so loud.

Bees help pollinate the flowers.

Bees are great.

Bees make delicious honey.

Main Idea

Read the paragraphs and answer the questions about them.

Remember that main ideas are what the paragraph or story is about. Sometimes they are stated, usually in the first sentence of a paragraph. Sometimes they are unstated and are more of a summary of the whole paragraph.

What is the main idea of this paragraph?
    a. Sometimes main ideas are stated.
    b. Main ideas are what the paragraph or story is about.
    c. Sometimes main ideas are unstated.

Have you ever watched an ice hockey game? It's completely legal to slam people into the boards as hard as possible. People get carried off the ice on stretchers from time to time. Concussions are common in the sport. Perhaps the danger is part of the excitement!

What is the main idea of this paragraph?
    a. Ice hockey can be dangerous.
    b. Have you ever watched an ice hockey game?
    c. Stretchers are involved in some hockey games.

Bristol has a beautiful flower garden. She has a huge array of flowers including roses and carnations. She takes great care of her flowers and waters them daily. Flowers fill her with joy.

What is the main idea of this paragraph?
    a. Bristol waters her flowers every day.
    b. Roses and carnations are types of flowers.
    c. Bristol really likes flowers.

My brother is so silly. His favorite food is mashed potatoes and ketchup. He wears a cape everywhere he goes. He twirls his hand above his head and runs down the hallways yelling, "Yeehaw!" multiple times a day. He's crazy, but I love him.

What is the main idea of this paragraph?
    a. I have a silly brother.
    b. My brother likes weird food combinations.
    c. My brother wears a cape everywhere he goes.

Writing

You are stranded on an island. You see something floating on the water headed toward shore. What is it? It can be anything you want it to be. Start your story with seeing it. What is it and how does it change life on the island forever?

_____

_____

_____

_____

_____

_____

_____

_____

Handwriting

Copy a great sentence from a book you are reading – something exciting, interesting, descriptive, or funny. Write carefully and neatly.

_____

_____

_____

Main Idea

Read the paragraphs and choose the main idea of each one.

Samuel is a kind-hearted kid. He donated his birthday money to the local homeless shelter when he learned he wasn't old enough to serve there. He swept his neighbor's porch when she twisted her ankle. He kept his dad from squishing a spider, convincing him to set it free outside instead. Samuel is a joy to be around.

What is the main idea of this paragraph?
  a. Samuel donated money to the homeless.
  b. Samuel is compassionate.
  c. Samuel likes spiders.

Apples are a great snack choice. They are full of fiber and vitamin C. The polyphenols in apples act as antioxidants. Everything from your bones to your brain can benefit from eating apples.

What is the main idea of this paragraph?
  a. Your bones can benefit from apples.
  b. Apples are good for you.
  c. Apples have polyphenols.

Writing

You are on the shore of your island and a bottle washes up with a message inside. What does the message say? Write a short story about it.

_____

_____

_____

_____

_____

_____

_____

_____

Spelling

Find the words in the puzzle below. Words can be found forward, backward, up, down, and diagonally.

```
B L U E D B N T V A M G G H J
W Z K D E S E R V E A N Y N O
S E C I L A L O Q K B I R T E
B E N T Y T A U B E L F Z K U
B I M B E S T B R I B F B G N
L V O C A B U L A R Y Z R F I
O B A G A I S E N Z L J A L T
C B A K E M R T G N T C R J N
K G T B K P U A R M L E E L O
B L U E D B N B V E T G G H C
W Z K Y G E A A O U N N Y N O
L E C I L A L B P K B G R T H
I E N T Y T E M L E H F T K I
C I M B E S O K R I B F B H A
N R S C N C S E I B E Z R F B
E B A G A I Y L T E I U Q L O
P B A K E M R N G N T C G J N
```

vocabulary	computer	pencil
trouble	continue	strength
helmet	deserve	quietly

Reading Comprehension

Read the story below and then answer the questions about the story.

The Fox and the Stork

At one time the Fox and the Stork were on visiting terms and seemed very good friends. So the Fox invited the Stork to dinner and for a joke put nothing before her but some soup in a very shallow dish. This the Fox could easily lap up, but the Stork could only wet the end of her long bill in it and left the meal as hungry as when she began. "I am sorry," said the Fox, "the soup is not to your liking."

"Pray do not apologize," said the Stork. "I hope you will return this visit, and come and dine with me soon." So a day was appointed when the Fox should visit the Stork; but when they were seated at table all that was for their dinner was contained in a very long-necked jar with a narrow mouth, in which the Fox could not insert his snout, so all he could manage to do was to lick the outside of the jar.

"I will not apologize for the dinner," said the Stork: "One bad turn deserves another."

What did the Fox serve for dinner?
a. stork
b. soup in a shallow dish
c. food in a long-necked jar
d. nothing

What did the Stork serve for dinner?
a. fox
b. soup in a shallow dish
c. food in a long-necked jar
d. nothing

Why did the Fox serve what he served?
a. as a joke
b. to be mean
c. they weren't friends
d. foxes don't like storks

What is the moral of the story?
a. Never trust a fox.
b. Storks get even.
c. Foxes and storks can't be friends.
d. One bad turn deserves another.

Writing

Write a dialogue between you and someone else. Just write dialogue – you talking back and forth with the other person. You could make it interesting and make the other person a character from a book you are reading. Put quotation marks around anything that is being said like this: *"I'm talking to you,"* I said. Start a new line each time a different person starts speaking.

_____

_____

_____

_____

_____

_____

_____

Writing

Copy the best sentence from a book you are reading. It can be the funniest, most interesting, most descriptive, most exciting — whatever you determine makes it the best sentence to copy. Write carefully and neatly.

_____

_____

_____

Verb Review

Look at each picture and come up with a verb you could use in a sentence involving the picture. For instance, for a picture of a ball you could write: kick, lob, throw, shoot, dribble, launch, sail, etc. Use a different verb for each picture.

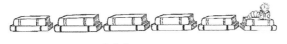

Writing

Pretend you are stranded on an island and someone has found you. Write a dialogue between you and the person. Would you consider staying? What would you ask about? What would you ask for? Write carefully and neatly.

_____

_____

_____

_____

_____

_____

_____

_____

Spelling

Write your spelling words on the lines below as they are read to you from the Parent's Guide. Learn from any spelling mistakes you make.

Quotation Marks

Add the missing punctuation to the sentences below by writing it in. Underline words that should be capitalized that aren't. Remember that quotations are punctuated like this:

"Let's have dinner."
"Let's have dinner," he said to her.
He said, "Let's have dinner."

Will you please turn on the TV   asked Dad

I can't find the remote anywhere   he added

I asked him   have you checked under the couch cushions

Sometimes Rex gets ahold of it and buries it there

Dad replied   that crazy dog! I didn't think of that

Aha! I found it   he exclaimed after checking the couch cushions

Now can you bring me a towel   he asked

He grimaced   he must have hidden it recently.
It's still covered in slobber

Comic

Make your own comic in the boxes below.

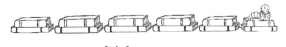

Writing

Choose someone about whom you'd like to write a biography. Today, write down five facts about the person. Your facts should answer the questions who, what, where, when, why, and how.

Person: _____

Fact 1: _____

_____

Fact 2: _____

_____

Fact 3: _____

_____

Fact 4: _____

_____

Fact 5: _____

_____

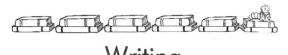

Writing

Find and write down five more facts about your person. Remember to be answering the questions who, what, where, when, why, and how.

Person: _____

Fact 6: _____

_____

Fact 7: _____

_____

Fact 8: _____

_____

Fact 9: _____

_____

Fact 10: _____

_____

Writing

Now organize your facts into the following categories: who/what, where/when, and why/how. If you have facts that don't fit those categories, use the last box. Write the fact number into the appropriate boxes below.

who/what

where/when

why/how

additional facts

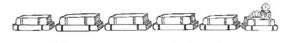

Quotation Marks

Add the missing punctuation to the sentences below by writing it in. Underline words that should be capitalized that aren't.

Where have you been, Mom   asked Jeffrey   we've been looking all over for you

I'm sorry   answered Mom   I needed to run an errand. But we can go to the park now

Okay, let's go   Rebecca stated   I want to get there before all of the swings are taken

Mom replied   okay. It's a beautiful day for a ride. Should we take the bikes

Yeah   both Jeffrey and Rebecca exclaimed in unison

Do we have any more sunscreen   asked Jeffrey

Mom answered   good call, Jeffrey. Let's get that on now so it can soak in before we get to the park

We should also bring some water   said Rebecca   it's hot out there today

You've both been listening during our health unit remarked Mom proudly

Writing

Write a story that includes dialogue. Be sure to use all of the quotation punctuation you've learned.

_____

_____

_____

_____

_____

_____

_____

_____

Writing

Form your who/what facts from lesson 48 into sentences using the hamburger below to help you write a paragraph. You need a topic sentence, three supporting detail sentences, and a conclusion sentence.

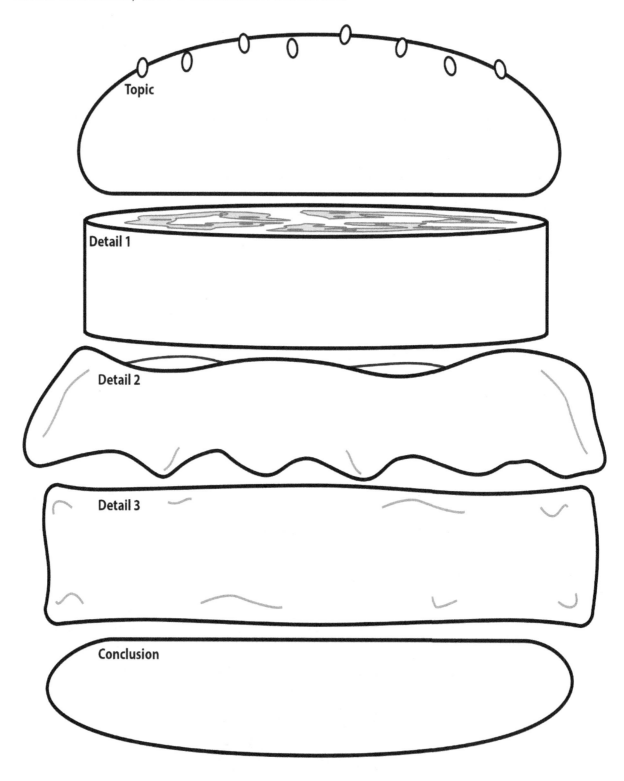

Topic

Detail 1

Detail 2

Detail 3

Conclusion

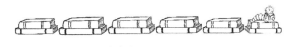

Writing

A **transition** is a word or phrase that takes the reader from one thought to another smoothly. Some examples of transitions are *finally, the next day, next, the following morning,* etc. Use a book you are reading and copy three sentences that use a transition.

_____

_____

_____

_____

_____

_____

Can you think of other transition words or phrases?

_____

_____

_____

_____

Writing

Form your where/when facts from lesson 48 into sentences using the hamburger below to help you write a paragraph. You need a topic sentence, three supporting detail sentences, and a conclusion sentence.

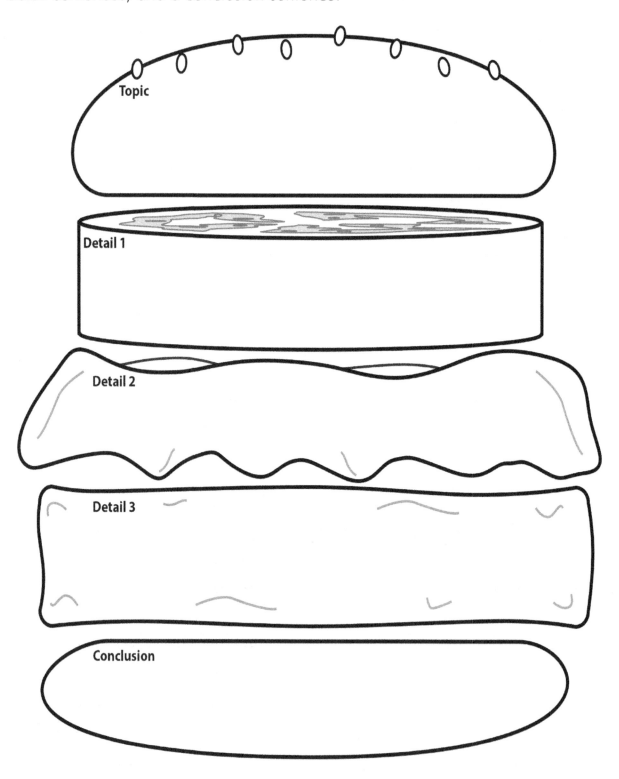

Topic

Detail 1

Detail 2

Detail 3

Conclusion

Quotation Marks

Cut out the following pieces and arrange them into different dialogues. Don't forget to use the rules you've learned.

" "	ait	" "	he	
said	?	.	.	.	w
asked	" "	W		
smiled	S	S	s	s
ight here	R	r	!	
he	He	he	.	.
ver there	o	O		
kay	,	,	" "	

(This page left intentionally blank)

Writing

Form your why/how facts from lesson 48 into sentences using the hamburger below to help you write a paragraph. You need a topic sentence, three supporting detail sentences, and a conclusion sentence.

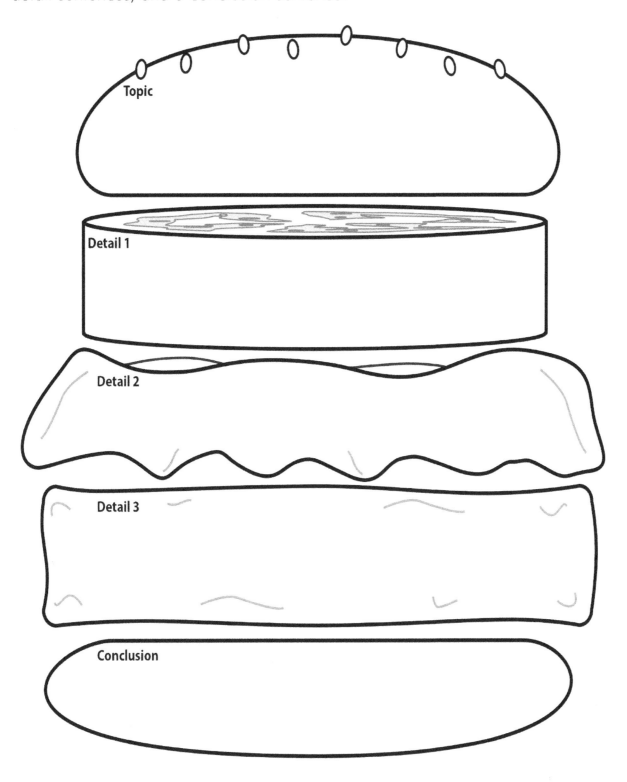

Topic

Detail 1

Detail 2

Detail 3

Conclusion

Writing

Write an introduction about your biography. This can be a shorter paragraph but should be at least three sentences long. This time instead of the first sentence being your main idea, the last sentence is going to be the main idea of your whole biography. It should be as specific as possible. Make your first sentence interesting. It should make people want to read your biography. An easy way to get people interested is by asking a question.

_____

_____

_____

_____

Proper Nouns

Which of the following nouns are proper? Do you remember?

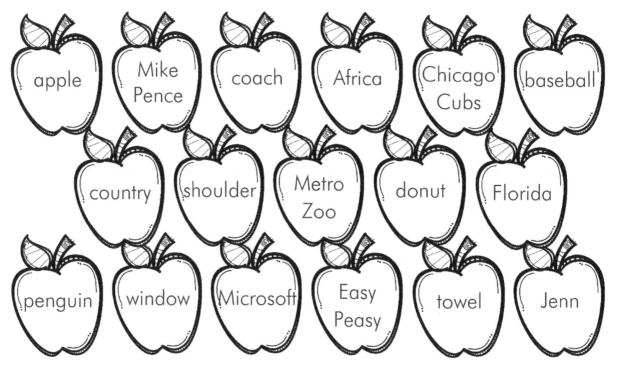

apple   Mike Pence   coach   Africa   Chicago Cubs   baseball

country   shoulder   Metro Zoo   donut   Florida

penguin   window   Microsoft   Easy Peasy   towel   Jenn

Writing

Write an account of your day yesterday. Include a sound word in every sentence, such as: creak, crash, burp, slurp, tweet, trickle, bump, shuffle, buzz, or any other sound word you can think of.

_____

_____

_____

_____

_____

_____

_____

_____

_____

achoo!   tick tock

choo choo

Writing

Write a conclusion paragraph for your biography. The first sentence should be your main idea again. Like your introduction, there should be at least three sentences. The last sentence should include the word "I." Tell what you think or feel about the person. Answer the question, "So what?" Tell why you wrote the essay.

_____

_____

_____

_____

Linking Verbs

Which of the following are linking verbs? Do you remember?

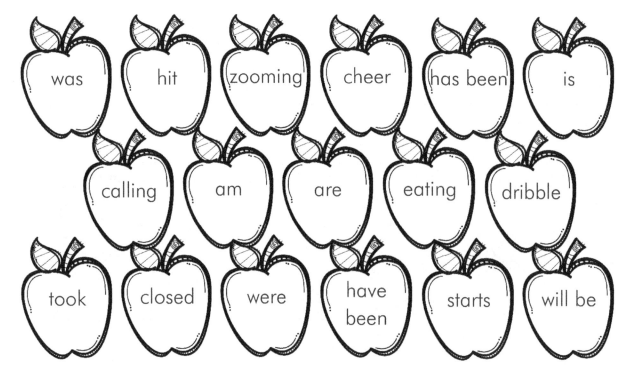

was   hit   zooming   cheer   has been   is

calling   am   are   eating   dribble

took   closed   were   have been   starts   will be

Nouns

Remember that **pronouns** take the place of nouns. Which of the words below are pronouns?

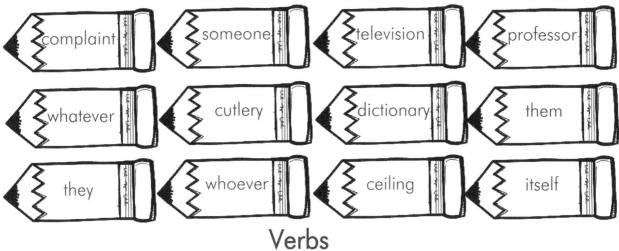

complaint   someone   television   professor

whatever   cutlery   dictionary   them

they   whoever   ceiling   itself

Verbs

Write in the verb choice that best matches the subject.

The girl _____.
ran/run

The boy has _____ it.
done/did

The dog had _____.
eaten/ate

The children _____.
sang/sung

The cherries _____ red.
was/were

The wind has _____.
blew/blown

Idioms

An **idiom** is a culturally used common phrase that has a figurative meaning. Can you match the idioms with their meanings?

barking up the wrong tree   right away

raining cats and dogs   easy

at the drop of a hat   not in the right place

hit the nail on the head   all of it

piece of cake   get it exactly right

whole nine yards   downpour

Writing

Write a letter to your mother, but write as someone from the time period you are studying in history. If you have to write your letter in hieroglyphics, so be it. ☺

_____

_____

_____

_____

_____

_____

_____

_____

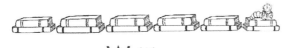

Writing

You are going to be taking your three hamburgers, your introduction, and your conclusion and putting them all together in a five paragraph essay. Make sure all of your paragraphs flow together. Try to make connections. Use connecting words to help make the paragraphs flow from one to the next. Write your introduction and who/what paragraphs today.

_____

_____

_____

_____

_____

_____

_____

_____

_____

_____

essay

Writing

Write your where/when and your why/how paragraphs of your essay today. Use your hamburgers. Make sure all of your paragraphs flow together. Try to make connections. Make your where/when paragraph from today connect to your who/what paragraph from yesterday. Use connecting words to help make the paragraphs flow from one to the next.

_____

_____

_____

_____

_____

_____

_____

_____

_____

essay

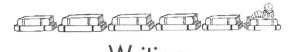

Writing

Today you need to write your conclusion paragraph. Then it's time to proofread. Read your biography out loud. Make sure the whole thing flows well. Make note of spots you stumble over and change them. Make sure there are long and short sentences. Do you have sentences with *and, but,* or *because*? Do you have exclamations and questions?

_____

_____

_____

_____

_____

Writing

Have others read your biography. Let them leave you feedback below. Great job writing a five paragraph essay!

I liked the essay because: _____

_____

My favorite fact was: _____

_____

I liked the essay because: _____

_____

My favorite fact was: _____

_____

I liked the essay because: _____

_____

My favorite fact was: _____

_____

Writing

Write a descriptive paragraph of a scene from a book you have been reading. Describe what you would see if you were there, what you would hear, what you would smell. Try to include at least one sentence each with a period, question mark, and exclamation point, and use at least one comma. When you're done, see if you can draw a picture of it in the box at the bottom.

_____

_____

_____

_____

_____

_____

Writing

Read your descriptive paragraph out loud. Fix any problems you hear. Now write an opening sentence that makes the reader interested in reading about the description. Then write a concluding sentence that contains a thought or feeling.

Opening: _____

_____

_____

Conclusion: _____

_____

_____

Practice being more descriptive. It can be a good day, or it can be a gorgeous, fantastic, or magnificent day. I can run, or I can bolt, sprint, or fly. Is that a tree, or is it a towering maple? Can you make these words more descriptive?

pretty _____

sleep _____

loud _____

flower _____

Writing

Write a summary of a book you have recently read. In one paragraph, tell the main characters, where they were, and what they did. Only use three to five sentences. Draw a scene from the book if you'd like.

_____

_____

_____

_____

_____

_____

_____

Writing

Using the same book you wrote about in lesson 67, write a paragraph telling the best thing about the book. Describe it and tell why you think it's the best thing. Again, write three to five sentences. Draw it if you'd like.

_____

_____

_____

_____

_____

_____

_____

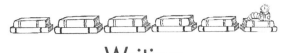
Writing

Using the same book you wrote about in lessons 67 and 68, now write a paragraph telling the worst thing about the book. Describe it and tell why you think it's the worst thing. Be descriptive. Again, write three to five sentences. Draw it if you'd like.

_____

_____

_____

_____

_____

_____

Writing

You now have the three middle paragraphs of a book report essay written. Today, write the introduction. In your introduction, write the author's name, the title of the book (be sure to write it in italics or underline it), and describe the book. How long is it? What words best describe it? Is it fun, adventurous, family, sad, exciting? Write three to five sentences. The last sentence should be the main idea you want to make about the book.

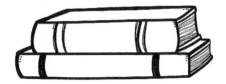

Writing

Write the conclusion to your book report essay. In your conclusion, tell what you think of the book. Would you recommend others read it? Would you read other books like it? Your last sentence should be a thought or feeling such as, *"I think..."* Write three to five sentences.

_____

_____

_____

_____

_____

_____

Editing Checklist

Read through your book report and fix any mistakes. Here is a list of things to keep track of as you edit. Aim for a check mark in each box.

Introduction

☐ My introduction begins with an attention grabber.
☐ My introduction has at least three sentences.
☐ My introduction ends with the main idea of my report.

Body

☐ The body of my report has at least three paragraphs.
☐ Each paragraph of the body starts with a topic sentence.
☐ Each paragraph of the body has at least three supporting sentences.
☐ Each paragraph of the body has a conclusion sentence.

Conclusion

☐ My conclusion has at least three sentences.
☐ My conclusion restates my main idea.
☐ My conclusion answers the question, "So what?"

Unity

☐ My report flows well and makes sense.
☐ My report uses transition words.
☐ My report is interesting.

Subject Matter

☐ My report has different sentences – short, long, compound, complex.
☐ My report uses descriptive words.
☐ All parts of my report support my main idea.

Grammar/Mechanics

☐ All words are spelled correctly.
☐ There are no grammatical mistakes.
☐ There are no punctuation errors.
☐ There are no fragments.
☐ There are no run-on sentences.

Feedback

Read your book report to or with your family. Let them leave feedback for you here.

I liked the report because: _____

_____

Something I learned was: _____

_____

Correct the punctuation, capitalization, and/or meaning of the following sentences.

Martin Mersenich was quoted as saying Did you know that it rains birds?

When asked for comment, the reporter said, "It remains to be seen whether or not the criminals will receive a life sentence".

We need to work fast. said Betty.

"I'm 100% sure!" Said thomas.

As a wise linguist once said, Comma splicing is bad, don't do it.

Adjectives

Underline the adjectives in the following sentences.

The bright light shone through the clean window.

Sally's purple scarf was made of soft cashmere.

We attended a delectable feast on that sunny Friday.

Our crazy family has a fabulous time together.

Her long, curly hair shimmered red in the sunshine.

The giggly baby lit up with a huge smile.

The sweltering heat sent us all inside for cool air.

Her bubbly bathwater smelled of fragrant lilacs.

His broken radio squawked out horrible sounds.

Have you been to the much-anticipated movie yet?

My favorite sweater is in the dirty laundry.

My annoying hiccups lasted forty-five minutes.

The friendly puppy licked my sticky fingers.

Formal Letter

Write a letter to the president. Use a formal letter writing format.

_____

_____

123 Any Street
Anytown, USA 01234

May 15, 2060

_____

President USA
1600 Pennsylvania Avenue
Washington, D.C. 20500

_____

Dear Mr. President:

_____

I just wanted to thank you for keeping the right to
homeschool such an important part of your presidency.
Every person should have the right to be educated in the
way that best fits them. I'm sure you're aware of the
many who've held your office before you who were
homeschooled. Even as late as FDR, homeschooling has
been an important part of our nation's history and
heritage. Keep up the good work!

Sincerely,
Sue Smith
Student

_____

_____

_____

_____

_____

_____

_____

_____

Adjectives

This fisherman wants a *delicious* dinner so he only wants you to color in the fish that contain adjectives.

careful

large

cord

skip

colorful

fluffy

bathtub

yellow

zebra

striped

snowy

straight

fetch

scary

crazy

jump

Writing

Write a fun story.

_____

_____

_____

_____

_____

_____

_____

_____

_____

Writing

Add LOTS of adjectives to your story from lesson 77. To help you brainstorm, make a list of ten adjectives here.

_____   _____

_____   _____

_____   _____

_____   _____

Make sure your story doesn't have three of the same type of sentence next to each other. Use words like *and, but, or, if, when,* or *because.* Use questions and exclamations. Can you think of ways to combine these sentences?

I like pizza. I like cheese. I like pepperoni. Maybe you like those things, too.

_____

_____

We went to the lake. It was cold outside. We swam anyway. It was a fun day.

_____

_____

Adjectives

Underline the adjectives in the sentences below. In addition to all you've learned about adjectives, keep in mind that the following words are always adjectives: a, an, the, my, our, your, their.

We went to the huge carnival and saw your brother there.

My best friend cooked a delicious meal.

What is your favorite book?

The girl with the blonde hair took my dessert.

Our bouncy ball flew over the privacy fence.

Which of the choices is an adjective? Some sentences have more than one!

You did a fantastic job on your spelling worksheet.
- ○ fantastic
- ○ you
- ○ job
- ○ worksheet

The three girls went to see the scary movie yesterday.
- ○ movie
- ○ three
- ○ went
- ○ scary

Her athletic ability was incredibly impressive.
- ○ ability
- ○ was
- ○ athletic
- ○ impressive

Our back pond was solid ice.
- ○ pond
- ○ our
- ○ back
- ○ solid

Speaking

Read your story out loud to an audience. Read it loudly and clearly. Use expression and make them laugh! Then get their feedback by having them fill out the page below.

I liked the story because:_____

_____

My favorite part was:_____

_____

I liked the story because:_____

_____

My favorite part was:_____

_____

I liked the story because:_____

_____

My favorite part was:_____

_____

Writing

You're going to be writing a new funny story. Today, draw your main character in the box below. Make a list of things that describe your character underneath the picture. Make sure you give your character a name and an age.

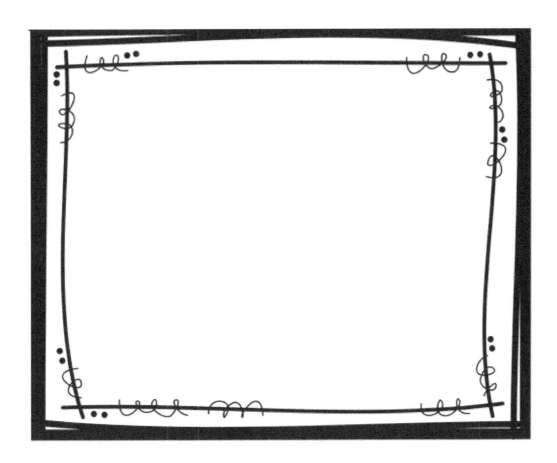

_____

_____

_____

_____

Writing

Draw or write what will happen at the beginning of your story. Where is your character at the beginning of the story? What's going on? Brainstorm and make notes for yourself.

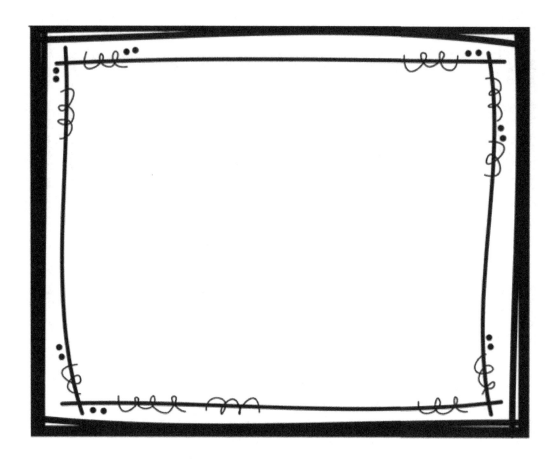

_____

_____

_____

_____

Writing

Draw or write what will happen in the middle and end of your story. What happens to your character? What makes it so funny? Brainstorm and make notes for yourself. Make a list.

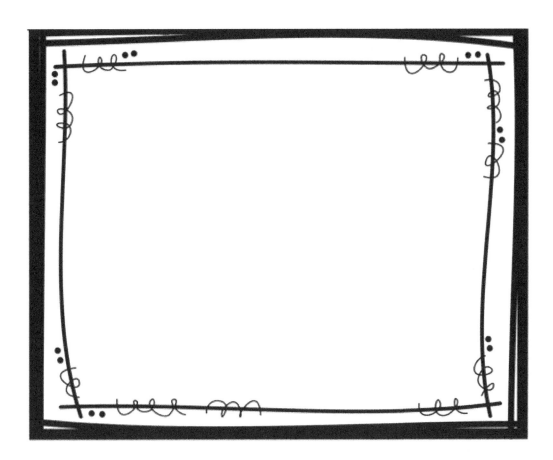

_____

_____

_____

_____

Parts of Speech

Let's review the parts of speech! Color all of the nouns blue. Color all of the verbs green. Color all of the adjectives red.

anxious

Eiffel Tower

go

cabinet

tasty

brawny

threw

nostril

ran

spleen

matchbox

steamy

come

Luke

cowboy

is

your

bravery

sit

defrost

peaceful

optimism

flashy

were

juicy

Writing

Begin writing your funny story. You can work on this through lesson 86. Use your notes from lesson 82. Be descriptive as you write.

_____

_____

_____

_____

_____

_____

_____

_____

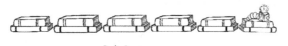
Writing

Finish writing your funny story. Remember to use lots of adjectives and different sentence types. Use your notes from lesson 83.

_____

_____

_____

_____

_____

_____

_____

_____

Feedback

Read your funny story to or with your family. Let them leave feedback for you here.

I liked the story because: _____

_____

My favorite part was: _____

_____

I liked the story because: _____

_____

My favorite part was: _____

_____

I liked the story because: _____

_____

My favorite part was: _____

_____

Spelling

Write your spelling words on the lines below as they are read to you from the Parent's Guide. Learn from any spelling mistakes you make.

_____   _____

_____   _____

_____   _____

_____   _____

_____   _____

_____   _____

Writing

Copy this sentence on the lines below. Then underline all the adjectives, circle the verbs, and draw a line through the nouns. *And as the three children went home up the hill, Peter hugging the engine, now quite its own self again, Bobbie told, with joyous leaps of the heart, the story of how she had been an Engine-burglar.*

_____

_____

_____

_____

Fill in the missing punctuation in the sentences below. Underline any words that should be capitalized that aren't.

It's almost my birthday   my sister practically shouted

We should go to the park today   Jeremy suggested

I can tell by the flowers trees and grass that it's spring.

My mom asked   where would you like to go for lunch

Come up with the best adjective you can to describe these nouns.

_____ hair   _____ day

_____ floor   _____ tree

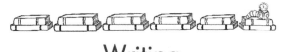

Writing

Write a short story about a stranger who showed up in your town. Who is he (or she) and how did he end up there?

_____

_____

_____

_____

_____

_____

_____

_____

Who's there?

Writing

This is a sentence from the book, *The Railway Children*: "She had never been a real heroine before, and the feeling was delicious." Write about something that would make you feel "delicious."

_____

_____

_____

_____

_____

_____

_____

_____

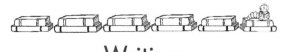

Writing

Describe one of your siblings or one of your parents. Don't just focus on what he or she looks like. Think about what they are like – how do they act? What makes them different or special?

_____

_____

_____

_____

_____

_____

_____

_____

Homophones

Homophones are words that sound alike but have different meanings. Can you match the word to the correct definition?

hare	a growth of hair around the face
hair	most important
mane	strands growing out of skin
main	an animal similar to a rabbit
through	in one side and out the other
threw	physical suffering or discomfort
pain	past tense of throw
pane	a single sheet of glass in a window
past	past tense of pass
passed	perceived with the ear
herd	a group of animals
heard	already happened

Writing

Copy this sentence. *"Well, then,"* said Bobbie, fumbling miserably, yet not without hope, *in her tightly stuffed pocket.*

_____

_____

_____

Look at the description in the sentence you copied. You can see what she did, how she did it, how she felt, and what it looked like. Write a sentence that gives a picture of what someone did, how they did it, how it felt, and how it looked.

_____

_____

_____

_____

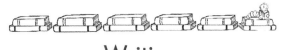

Writing

Write a short story using at least two homophones, but try to use as many as possible. If you use more than two, get a high five and/or a hug.

_____

_____

_____

_____

_____

_____

_____

_____

Word Builder

How many words can you make from the letters in the box below? Only use
letters that are adjacent to each other (see the example).

B	R	A	R	D	A	S	P
N	I	T	I	C	K	A	D
M	S	E	S	A	T	B	O
Z	B	E	T	E	G	N	H
M	C	I	Q	L	R	D	S
A	P	E	E	H	A	C	Y
U	J	P	A	L	Y	O	D
K	R	V	O	E	G	A	D
D	F	I	B	J	T	Q	F
N	O	N	U	T	Z	E	T
C	W	E	K	A	S	C	L
M	B	A	K	G	R	N	E
J	M	D	W	A	F	G	W
L	A	I	T	S	O	E	P

brains

Spelling

Write your spelling words on the lines below as they are read to you from the Parent's Guide. Learn from any spelling mistakes you make.

_____   _____

_____   _____

_____   _____

_____   _____

_____   _____

_____   _____

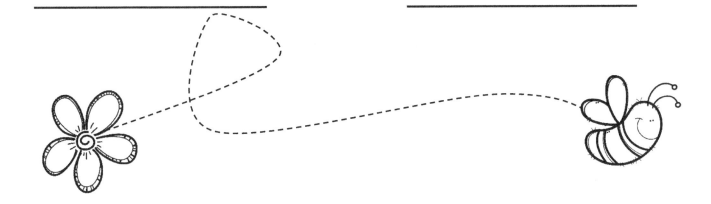

Nouns

Can you identify the different noun types? Choose the answer that best describes the word given by filling in the circle beside it.

apples
◯ singular noun   ◯ plural noun

◯ proper noun   ◯ compound noun

Pepsi
◯ singular noun   ◯ plural noun

◯ abstract noun   ◯ proper noun

sunset
◯ abstract noun   ◯ plural noun

◯ proper noun   ◯ compound noun

anxiety
◯ abstract noun   ◯ plural noun

◯ collective noun   ◯ proper noun

vest
◯ singular noun   ◯ plural noun

◯ proper noun   ◯ abstract noun

family
◯ singular noun   ◯ proper noun

◯ collective noun   ◯ plural noun

mice
◯ singular noun   ◯ plural noun

◯ abstract noun   ◯ proper noun

White House
◯ singular noun   ◯ plural noun

◯ abstract noun   ◯ proper noun

Alyssa
◯ singular noun   ◯ plural noun

◯ proper noun   ◯ compound noun

team
◯ collective noun   ◯ plural noun

◯ abstract noun   ◯ proper noun

swimming pool
◯ abstract noun   ◯ plural noun

◯ proper noun   ◯ compound noun

perseverance
◯ concrete noun   ◯ plural noun

◯ abstract noun   ◯ proper noun

Idioms

Do you know what these idioms mean? Fill in the circle next to the answer you think is correct. Then check your answers and see how you did.

a chip on your shoulder
- ○ acting grumpy because you're upset about something
- ○ dropping food on your shirt
- ○ breaking a bone

a dime a dozen
- ○ something that only comes in sets of ten or twelve
- ○ something that is very common and easy to get
- ○ something that is cheaply made

tip of the iceberg
- ○ something that sticks up out of nowhere
- ○ only a small part of the whole issue
- ○ something sharp

all bark and no bite
- ○ someone who is angry because they are hungry
- ○ a loud dog
- ○ someone who has a lot of words but no actions to back it up

break a leg
- ○ have need of first aid
- ○ good luck
- ○ to be accident prone

all ears
- ○ ready to listen
- ○ not having a sense of smell
- ○ an elephant

Crossword

Can you fill in the following crossword puzzle? Each matching number equals a matching letter. (For instance, if you thought the "s" belonged in number 1, you would fill in all the number 1s with that letter.) Can you figure it out? Only use letters from the box at the top. They are capitalized for readability. If you need help, look at the hints provided.

F	G	L	N	S	T	W	V

Across:
3: move back and forth

Down:
5: go away

Copywork

Copy this sentence: *Once on a dark winter's day, when the yellow fog hung so thick and heavy in the streets of London that the lamps were lighted and the shop windows blazed with gas as they do at night, an odd-looking little girl sat in a cab with her father and was driven rather slowly through the big thoroughfares.* Draw a box around all the nouns. Underline all the adjectives. Circle the verbs.

_____

_____

_____

_____

_____

_____

_____

This is a good sentence because it tells what is happening, describes it, and makes you feel it. What types of feelings does this sentence produce?

_____

The **adverbs** in this sentence are "rather slowly." **Adverbs** are words that describe verbs, adjectives, and other adverbs. What is the verb being described by rather slowly?

_____

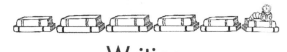

Writing

Read this sentence: *When Sara entered the school-room the next morning everybody looked at her with wide, interested eyes.* List the nouns, adjectives and verbs separately.

Nouns: _____

Verbs: _____

Adjectives: _____

Write a sentence that shows (not tells) us that the people in the room are scared.

_____

_____

_____

Write a sentence that shows (not tells) us that the people in the room are happy.

_____

_____

_____

Writing

Read: *On that first morning, when Sara sat at Miss Minchin's side, aware that the whole school-room was devoting itself to observing her, she had noticed very soon one little girl, about her own age, who looked at her very hard with a pair of light, rather dull, blue eyes.* List the nouns, pronouns, adjectives, and verbs separately.

Nouns: _____

_____

Pronouns: _____

_____

Verbs: _____

Adjectives: _____

_____

Write a "when" sentence. (Example: *When I entered the room, I was surprised by what I saw.*)

_____

Add a description to your sentence. (Example: *When I entered the room, the one our family spends most of its time in, I was surprised by what I saw.*)

_____

Add a clause to the end of your sentence. Don't forget to section off your clauses with commas. (Example: *When I entered the room, the one our family spends most of its time in, I was surprised by what I saw, something I will never forget.*)

_____

_____

_____

Writing

Write a long sentence with at least six adjectives and at least two verbs. Start out "When…," Don't forget the comma! Here's an example: *When the five squirmy children finally rustle out from under their warm and wrinkled covers, they immediately rush for the kitchen with one important question on their eager lips, "What's for breakfast?"* Don't forget to section off your clauses with commas.

_____

_____

_____

_____

_____

What are your adjectives?

_____

_____

What are your verbs?

_____

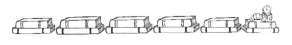

Writing

Read this sentence: *Of course the greatest power Sara possessed and the one which gained her even more followers than her luxuries and the fact that she was "the show pupil," the power that Lavinia and certain other girls were most envious of, and at the same time most fascinated by in spite of themselves, was her power of telling stories and of making everything she talked about seem like a story, whether it was one or not.* Write a sentence in a similar fashion. Start with, "The thing…" I'm most proud of, or that makes me happiest, or I'm most scared of…

_____

_____

Now look at the bold sentence again. The thing that makes Sara the most popular is her story telling. But it doesn't just say that. What comes in between? Add an "in between" in your sentence. Use commas to section off your clauses.

_____

_____

Write a short, fun story, a wonderfully inventive story like Sara would tell. Try to use long sentences with multiple clauses.

_____

_____

_____

_____

_____

_____

Parts of Speech

Color the noun apples blue. Color the verb apples red. Color the adjective apples green.

Now write a short story about yourself. Use at least 5 adjectives that describe you.

_____

_____

_____

_____

_____

_____

Adverbs

Write 5 adverbs describing how you can do your school work.

_____

_____

Now write 5 adverbs describing how you can treat your family members.

_____

_____

Spelling

See how many words you can come up with using the grid of letters below. Only use letters that are adjacent to one another as you have done in the past. This grid is smaller, can you still do it?

C	A	S	E
B	S	L	F
O	T	R	U
P	I	M	E

_____   _____   _____

_____   _____   _____

_____   _____   _____

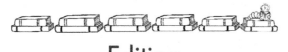

Editing

Fix the errors in the paragraph below by underlining the words that need to be capitalized and correcting the punctuation mistakes.

youve written a lot of short stories so far this year. Have you used lots of adverbs and adjectives to make your stories descriptive. Are your words all spelled correctly. Sometimes spelling mistakes are hard to see. be sure to read carefully! My mom would always ask me did you punctuate your quotations correctly? Yes, mom   I would answer after checking to be sure. after youve fixed your changes, it can be helpful to have someone else read over your story as well. dont take suggestions as criticisms. Always learn from your mistakes?

*Complete your three autobiography pages at the back of the book.

Good vs. Well

The word *good* is an adjective. It will describe a noun. The word *well* is an adverb. It will describe a verb, adjective, or other adverb. Can you fill in the blanks below with the correct word?

My grandma cooks really _____.

Her picture was drawn so _____ I felt like I was in it.

Those donuts tasted really _____.

A hot shower feels _____ on my muscles.

Do you perform _____ under pressure?

Our plans sound _____ to me.

Our TV isn't working very _____ right now.

A lot of people think *Star Wars* is a _____ series.

How _____ are you doing on your school work?

My mother is feeling _____ after being sick.

The children put on a _____ play at church.

How _____ do you know your best friend?

Writing

Write a pretend day from your life. You are the star character. It takes place in your home or another place you are at regularly, but it's a made up story that never happened.

Writing

Look at this sentence: *There was, however, one place from which one could see all the splendor of them: the piles of red or gold clouds in the west; or the purple ones edged with dazzling brightness; or the little fleecy, floating ones, tinged with rose-color and looking like flights of pink doves scurrying across the blue in a great hurry if there was a wind.* Write a sentence with "however" in the middle. Put a comma before and after it. Note that in this sentence, the part before "however" is a complete sentence with a subject and a verb. The part after is not – there is no verb. Can you write a sentence like this where the words after the "however" could not be their own sentence? Here's another, shorter example: *I got some of my work done, however, just my schoolwork and not my chores.*

_____

_____

_____

The word *only* can be used as an adverb. If you used *only* in the sentence you just wrote and it's not describing a noun, underline it and write **adverb** above or below it. Write one sentence with at least two adverbs in it. If you use more, get a high five and/or hug.

_____

_____

_____

*Complete your two autobiography pages at the back of the book.

Spelling

Can you correctly spell the words missing from these sentences? Hint: they all start with the letter b.

I knew he was the sheriff when I saw his __ __ __ __ __.

I need to fill in the __ __ __ __ __ in this sentence.

The __ __ __ __ __ __ asked us for money.

I took my shovel and __ __ __ __ __ __ to the beach.

May I __ __ __ __ __ __ your pen? Mine ran out of ink.

He blew a large __ __ __ __ __ __ with his gum.

Writing

Look at this sentence: *When one lives in a row of houses, it is interesting to think of the things which are being done and said on the other side of the wall of the very rooms one is living* in. Let's write another "when" sentence. Start with "When…" At the end of the clause don't forget the comma.

_____

_____

_____

*Complete your four autobiography pages at the back of the book.

Semicolons

Look at this sentence: *There were days on which Sara tramped through snow when she went on her errands; there were worse days when the snow melted and combined itself with mud to form slush; there were others when the fog was so thick that the lamps in the street were lighted all day and London looked as it had looked the afternoon, several years ago, when the cab had driven through the thoroughfares with Sara tucked up on its seat, leaning against her father's shoulder.* It uses **semicolons** (;). They are used in place of periods when you don't want to end the sentence. This long sentence reads like a list. The author could have used a period before each "there were." But since all of these sentences were connected, she combined them using **semicolons**. Find two ;s in that sentence.

Now write your own sentence with a **semicolon**. You will write two sentences and then use a ; instead of a . For example, here are three related sentences like in the book: *I want to go to the park and to the playground; I want to go to the mall and to the food court; I want to do too many things.* You try. Write two sentences that are related. Instead of ending the first sentence with a period, end it with a semicolon and then write the second sentence, beginning it with a lowercase letter unless it is a name.

_____

_____

Can you write another pair of sentences with a semicolon?

_____

_____

*Complete your eight autobiography pages at the back of the book.

Writing

Write a short story. Use at least one proper noun, five adjectives, three adverbs, the word "however," and a semicolon. Get a high five and/or hug if you include more than that, or if you include a sentence that begins with "when." Don't get bogged down with the rules. Just start writing! You can always go back and add in the things you missed.

_____

_____

_____

_____

_____

_____

_____

_____

Paragraphs

Paragraphs make text easier to read. Each paragraph only deals with one topic or subject. Answer the questions below about paragraphs.

Which of these is a proper paragraph?

I went on a camping trip yesterday. I had a tent, sleeping bag, and flashlight. It was a fun night in the woods.	Sleeping bag	I had a tent, sleeping bag, and flashlight.

How can you use punctuation to show the start of a new paragraph?

Use commas	Indent and start on a new line.	Write in complete sentences.

What would be a reason to start a new paragraph?

A new page	A new sentence	A new topic

In a conversation, what's another reason to start a new paragraph?

A new speaker	A new sentence	It's getting too long

Which of these is split into paragraphs in the right place?

I went on a camping trip yesterday. I had a tent, sleeping bag, and flashlight. The next day, I went home. My bed felt soft.	I went on a camping trip yesterday. I had a tent, sleeping bag, and flashlight. The next day, I went home. My bed felt soft.	I went on a camping trip yesterday. I had a tent, sleeping bag, and flashlight. The next day, I went home. My bed felt soft.

*Complete your two autobiography pages at the back of the book.

Spelling

Can you correctly spell the words missing from these sentences? Hint: these words all have the "shun" sound at the end.

We took up a __ __ __ __ __ __ __ __ __ __ __ to raise money for the new library.

The road __ __ __ __ __ __ __ __ __ __ __ __ __ for the new bridge made traffic back up for miles.

"One half" is known as a __ __ __ __ __ __ __ __.

He did a complete __ __ __ __ __ __ __ __ __ __ of the building to make sure it was safe.

The presidential __ __ __ __ __ __ __ __ __ draws lots of voters every four years.

Adverbs

Find four adverbs in this sentence. Adverbs answer the question, how. *She climbed on a chair, very cautiously raised the skylight, and peeped out. It had been snowing all day, and on the snow, quite near her, crouched a tiny, shivering figure, whose small black face wrinkled itself piteously at sight of her.*

_____   _____

_____   _____

Editing

Using a comma and a conjunction such as *and, but, for, or, nor, so,* or *yet,* combine these pairs of sentences into one long sentence.

I went to the store. Then I went to the bank.

_____

_____

I can't get out of bed. My mom is taking care of me.

_____

_____

It is raining today. You need an umbrella.

_____

_____

Fill in the blank with a more interesting or more descriptive word than the one that is given.

The weather is _____ today.
            (nice)

My dog likes to _____ outside.
            (walk)

The _____ was licking its paws.
        (cat)

That tree is _____.
            (big)

*Complete your two autobiography pages at the back of the book.

Word Search

Find the words in the word search below. These words are from the book *A Little Princess* from Easy Peasy's level 4 reading. Words can be found vertically, horizontally, and diagonally.

```
U  I  G  T  A  H  Q  H  D  N  C  W  M  Y  C  L  Q
B  M  J  K  W  J  T  E  E  Z  H  R  E  J  X  Q  L
Y  P  Y  B  R  W  U  Y  Y  C  E  T  J  A  O  I  D
Q  U  W  V  U  Z  D  D  M  T  A  D  U  Y  C  M  E
Q  D  C  F  X  O  F  C  I  L  S  I  L  L  E  P  X
P  E  S  H  S  H  B  O  O  U  Z  T  V  R  I  E  T
A  N  U  U  H  Y  N  S  O  M  N  P  U  S  E  R  E
L  T  Q  P  V  N  N  R  T  E  I  T  W  I  Y  T  R
P  B  H  W  O  O  U  O  N  I  R  G  E  M  G  I  I
I  P  Y  C  C  T  Y  I  O  E  N  S  O  O  O  N  T
T  J  E  S  P  K  T  B  P  X  A  A  C  I  V  E  Y
A  R  I  A  V  N  R  A  S  X  Y  O  T  U  T  N  N
T  D  R  B  O  J  S  O  R  D  I  D  B  E  F  C  B
I  Y  R  C  Z  C  M  Y  V  O  V  B  U  Y  W  E  K
N  Z  N  D  E  U  D  R  E  B  H  D  U  J  Z  L  Q
G  I  J  M  K  X  W  B  R  W  C  E  Z  E  Z  W  U
P  R  E  C  I  P  I  T  A  T  E  L  Y  L  C  Y  W
```

dexterity	disconsolate	impudent
aperture	precipitately	incontinently
sordid	palpitating	obstinate
rapturous	reconnoiter	impertinence

Adjectives

This story used all the wrong adjectives! Can you replace the negative adjectives with positive ones from the box? Use all of the adjectives once. Some can go in more than one place.

| wonderful | available | exhilarating | pleasant | perfect |
| cheerful | satisfied | delighted | amazing | sunny | terrific |

The girls at the park were _____. The swings
                                (unhappy)

were _____. The sky was _____
         (broken)   (gloomy)

and the air was _____, making for a
                         (crisp)

_____ day for outside play. The park was
     (miserable)

full of _____ and _____ kids.
            (grumpy)   (disgruntled)

"This is so _____ and _____,"
                  (boring)   (exhausting)

the girls said as they took in the scene. "What a

_____ day!"
    (horrible)

*Complete your two autobiography pages at the back of the book.

Parts of Speech

The barrel at the end of each sentence tells you what part of speech to look for in the sentence. Color in all the apples that should go in that sentence's barrel based on the context of the sentence. Some of them are tricky so pay attention!

Let's go for a relaxing swim in the pool.

 go relaxing  swim  pool

 verbs

She went for a run to the bookstore yesterday.

 she  run  bookstore  yesterday

 nouns

The little girl was overly happy.

 The  little  overly  happy

 adjectives

The very grumpy man was rudely pouting.

 very  grumpy  rudely  pouting

 adverbs

She picked up a ball and threw it hard.

 She  up  and  it

 pronouns

Book Review

You are going to write a book review about a book you've recently read. Today, choose your book and pick some of the questions below to answer.

- What was the book about? Tell something about the main character. What happens to them in the story?
- What was your favorite part? Why was it your favorite?
- What sort of book was it? Biography? Nonfiction? Fantasy? Classic novel?
- Did you like the book? Why or why not? What were the best parts of the book? Did parts of the book make you laugh?
- Were you able to imagine yourself as part of the story? If so, what about it made it easy to do that?
- What sort of people would like this book? Would you recommend it to a certain age or gender?

_____

_____

_____

_____

_____

_____

_____

Book Review

Today, organize your answers from lesson 121 into a paragraph. Your first and last sentence should tell your overall opinion of the book. The middle should tell a bit of what the book is about and the good and bad parts of it. Keep it brief.

_____

_____

_____

_____

_____

_____

_____

_____

_____

_____

Parts of Speech

Identify the part of speech of the underlined word and write it on the blank.

Our whole family fit in the <u>enormous</u> booth. _____

The <u>overly</u> luxurious spa weekend was relaxing. _____

"I am excited for Christmas," she <u>said</u> eagerly. _____

The large <u>church</u> loomed before us on the hill. _____

His pile of books was bigger than <u>mine</u>. _____

"We <u>are</u> hungry," stated the children. _____

Her <u>surprise</u> party was a spectacular success. _____

Come <u>hastily</u> to see the baby bird try to fly! _____

I'm tired. Can we go home <u>soon</u>? _____

The thunderstorm filled my dog with <u>anxiety</u>. _____

The cover made the book <u>seem</u> boring. _____

Put the book over <u>there</u> on my nightstand. _____

That bathroom isn't going to clean <u>itself</u>. _____

I find chocolate to be <u>simply</u> irresistible. _____

*Complete your one autobiography page at the back of the book.

Editing

Underline the words that need to be capitalized and add in any missing punctuation to these sentences.

I can't wait   my mom exclaimed eagerly

We went to seattle in the fall but it rained our whole trip

Peter asked   have you had lunch yet

Sheila Becky and Sarah joined the soccer team

The traffic is bad on lake street   she informed me

Fill in the blank with a more interesting or more descriptive word than the one that is given.

The flowers are _____.
(pretty)

Stacey _____ the ball.
(threw)

The mouse _____ the cheese.
(ate)

"Get out of my room!" she _____.
(said)

*Complete your one autobiography page at the back of the book.

Biography

Interview someone in your family to help you write a biography about them. Ask them to describe themselves. Ask them for a word that describes them. Ask for three stories that show why they are that way. Take notes below as you interview your family member.

_____

_____

_____

_____

_____

_____

_____

_____

Biography

Today, write the first middle paragraph of your essay. The body, or three middle paragraphs of your essay will tell the three story examples from your interview. For this paragraph, choose one of the story examples. Like with the hamburger worksheets, the first sentence is your main idea. For example: *One of the ways my grandfather was creative was by painting.* (Creative is the word that describes him.) Then you would tell about his painting. Then write a final sentence after you tell the story. For example: *One of his paintings is hanging in my room, and I love to look at it.* Write your first paragraph.

_____

_____

_____

_____

_____

Biography

Today, write the second middle paragraph of your essay. The body, or three middle paragraphs of your essay will tell the three story examples from your interview. For this paragraph, choose another of the story examples. Like with the hamburger worksheets, the first sentence is your main idea. Use a **transition** word for this paragraph. For example: **Another** *way my grandfather was creative was by playing the clarinet.* Then you would tell about his music. Then write a final sentence after you tell the story. For example: *I use his old clarinet and am learning to play it myself.* Write your second paragraph.

_____

_____

_____

_____

_____

Biography

Today, write the third middle paragraph of your essay. The body, or three middle paragraphs of your essay will tell the three story examples from your interview. For this paragraph, choose another of the story examples. Like with the hamburger worksheets, the first sentence is your main idea. Use a **transition** word again for this paragraph. For example: **A final** *way my grandfather was creative was by inventing.* Then you would tell about his inventions. Then write a final sentence after you tell the story. For example: *I think he was a genius in the things he invented.* Write your third paragraph.

_____

_____

_____

_____

_____

Biography

Today, write the conclusion to your essay. The first sentence should say the main idea of your essay. For example: *My grandfather was a creative genius.* In your last sentence, compare or contrast yourself to the person you wrote about. For example: *My grandfather was creative in so many ways, and although I don't have the same talents as he did, I like to think I'm creative just like he was.* Your conclusion should have at least three sentences.

_____

_____

_____

_____

_____

Grammar Review

Answer the questions below.

This is a person, place, thing, or idea.

noun   verb   adjective   adverb

This describes a noun.

noun   verb   adjective   adverb

This describes verbs and adjectives.

noun   verb   adjective   adverb

This connects the two parts of a compound sentence.

suffix   conjunction   synonym   antonym

"Pittsburgh" is an example of this.

proper noun   pronoun   linking verb   action verb

"Overly expensive" is an example of this.

adverb describing an adjective   homonym
compound sentence   adjective describing a noun

A sentence that makes a command is this type of sentence.

interrogative   declarative   exclamatory   imperative

Which part of speech is the underlined word: "I am hungry."?

noun   verb   adjective   adverb

Biography

Today, write the introduction to your essay. This time instead of the first sentence being your main idea, the last sentence is going to be your main idea. Your introduction should be at least three sentences long. Your first sentence should be interesting. It should make people want to read your biography. An easy way to get people interested is by asking a question. For example: *Have you ever known a genius? Genius comes in many forms. There are math geniuses and writer geniuses. My grandfather's genius was in his creativity.*

_____

_____

_____

_____

_____

Editing Checklist

Read through your biography and fix any mistakes. Here is your editing checklist again. Remember to aim for a check mark in each box.

Introduction
- ☐ My introduction begins with an attention grabber.
- ☐ My introduction has at least three sentences.
- ☐ My introduction ends with the main idea of my essay.

Body
- ☐ The body of my essay has at least three paragraphs.
- ☐ Each paragraph of the body starts with a topic sentence.
- ☐ Each paragraph of the body has at least three supporting sentences.
- ☐ Each paragraph of the body has a conclusion sentence.

Conclusion
- ☐ My conclusion has at least three sentences.
- ☐ My conclusion restates my main idea.
- ☐ My conclusion answers the question, "So what?"

Unity
- ☐ My essay flows well and makes sense.
- ☐ My essay uses transition words.
- ☐ My essay is interesting.

Subject Matter
- ☐ My essay has different sentences – short, long, compound, complex.
- ☐ My essay uses descriptive words.
- ☐ All parts of my essay support my main idea.

Grammar/Mechanics
- ☐ All words are spelled correctly.
- ☐ There are no grammatical mistakes.
- ☐ There are no punctuation errors.
- ☐ There are no fragments.
- ☐ There are no run-on sentences.

Capitalization

Underline the words in the sentences that should be capitalized.

Will you be coming home for christmas this year?

Both english and french are spoken by canadians.

i went to target to look for some jif peanut butter.

my mother is a graduate of trevecca nazarene university.

i can't believe mrs. mogg moved to santa fe!

We all went to holiday world in santa claus, indiana.

Spelling

Join the syllable given with a syllable from the box to make a two syllable word. They are each used only one time.

-day	-ment	-dle	-ful	-dle	-ner	-low	-lete

ath_____   mid_____

fig_____   to_____

din_____   rest_____

yel_____   han_____

Writing

Choose an event in your life to write about. Start writing. Write the first paragraph.
Start with an interesting sentence! Your first paragraph should tell a bit about what
the story is going to be, like telling the main idea in a non-fiction essay.

_____

_____

_____

_____

_____

_____

Writing

Write more of your story.

_____

_____

_____

_____

_____

_____

_____

_____

_____

_____

Writing

When we write non-fiction, we finish by restating our main idea. In a story, you finish where you start. You close the circle. Don't leave your readers hanging! Finish writing your story. Close the circle by connecting the ending back to the beginning.

_____

_____

_____

_____

_____

_____

_____

Editing Checklist

Read through your story and fix any mistakes. Here again is the list of things to keep track of as you edit. Aim for a check mark in each box.

Introduction
- [ ] My introduction begins with an attention grabber.
- [ ] My introduction has at least three sentences.
- [ ] My introduction ends with the main idea of my story.

Body
- [ ] The body of my story has at least three paragraphs.
- [ ] Each paragraph of the body starts with a topic sentence.
- [ ] Each paragraph of the body has at least three supporting sentences.
- [ ] Each paragraph of the body has a conclusion sentence.

Conclusion
- [ ] My conclusion has at least three sentences.
- [ ] My conclusion restates my main idea.
- [ ] My conclusion answers the question, "So what?" or closes the circle.

Unity
- [ ] My story flows well and makes sense.
- [ ] My story uses transition words.
- [ ] My story is interesting.

Subject Matter
- [ ] My story has different sentences – short, long, compound, complex.
- [ ] My story uses descriptive words.
- [ ] All parts of my story support my main idea.

Grammar/Mechanics
- [ ] All words are spelled correctly.
- [ ] There are no grammatical mistakes.
- [ ] There are no punctuation errors.
- [ ] There are no fragments.
- [ ] There are no run-on sentences.

Writing

Write a main idea sentence for the chapter you read today. If you didn't read a chapter today, you'll have to use something else like a children's book you know well or some other story.

_____

_____

_____

Adverbs

Color in the basketballs below that contain adverbs.

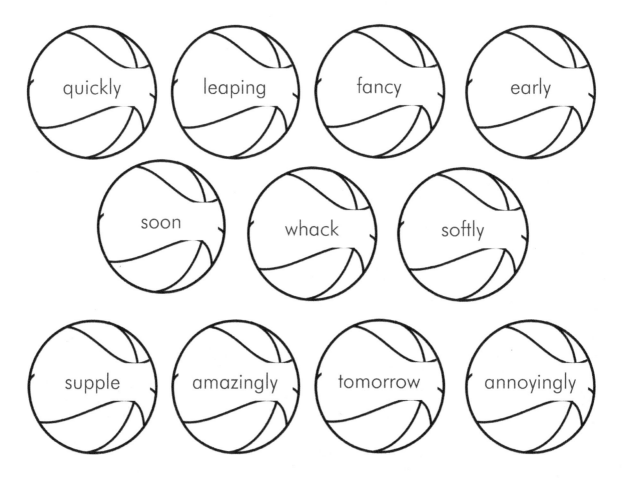

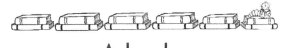

Adverbs

Adverbs can tell **how** something happened. *Sally <u>accidentally</u> dropped her doll in the puddle.* Adverbs can tell **when** something happened. *Sally dropped her doll <u>yesterday</u>.* Adverbs can tell **where** something happened. *Sally dropped it <u>here</u>.* Read these sentences. An action verb is in bold type. Underline the adverb that describes the bolded verbs.

We quickly **ran** to the mini mart for a snack.

Sandra, will you please **come** here?

We **went** to the park yesterday.

She cautiously **maneuvered** into traffic.

Her daughter **prayed** beautifully before they all ate.

They will **go** to the library soon.

He carefully **wrote** in his best handwriting.

The dog next door always **barks**.

We frantically **searched** for the lost set of keys.

Let's **make** plans tomorrow.

Bonus: My dad **snored** loudly as he **slept** dreamlessly.

Writing

Write an interesting first sentence for a paragraph in your reading today. Then write a main idea sentence for the chapter you read today. If you didn't have a reading assignment today, use something you've read recently or a book you know well.

_____

_____

_____

_____

_____

_____

Adverbs

Underline the adverbs that describe the bolded words below.

The big, fluffy dog was really **soft**.

I never **see** stars in our bright city sky.

We are **going** to the zoo tomorrow.

Main Idea

Can you answer these questions about a written piece's **main idea**? Check your answers when you're finished and review what you missed so you can learn.

A main idea is…
   a.   the general topic
   b.   the specific point being made about the topic
   c.   a supporting detail

The main idea is reinforced by…
   a.   supporting details
   b.   statements of opinion
   c.   good grammar

What might be the main idea in an essay on smoking?
   a.   smoking
   b.   cigarettes
   c.   smoking is bad for your health

Where is the main idea most often in a paragraph?
   a.   in the first sentence
   b.   in the middle
   c.   in the last sentence

What's a good way to find the main idea of something you're reading?
   a.   ask yourself general questions about what you've read
   b.   only read the piece once
   c.   memorize the piece

Which statement is true about main ideas?
   a.   they are always factual
   b.   they need to have good supporting details
   c.   they should be stated first

Inferences

An **inference** is a guess you can make based on the information you have. It's what some people call reading between the lines. What can you infer from the following passages?

Sheila shivered and checked the thermostat. She turned the heat up a notch and pulled her blanket tighter around herself. She checked that the fire in the fireplace had plenty of kindling to keep burning.

    a.   Sheila was good at solving problems.

    b.   Sheila was cold.

    c.   It was summer.

I jumped into the pool, a grin lighting up my face.

    a.   I was being chased by bees.

    b.   Someone was in trouble and I was a lifeguard.

    c.   I was having fun at the pool.

Cam flipped through his scrapbook and smiled. He saw the group picture in front of the Leaning Tower of Pisa. He grinned at the picture of himself in front of Buckingham Palace. He could almost smell the pastries as he gazed on the photo of the Eiffel Tower. It had been a great summer.

    a.   Cam likes pictures.

    b.   Cam likes smiling.

    c.   Cam took a summer trip to Europe.

I saw a flash of light. Shortly after that, I heard a rumble. The sun seems to have disappeared. Can you predict what might happen next?

    a.   I will see a great fireworks show in the sky.

    b.   I will go to sleep because it is nighttime.

    c.   It will rain.

Writing

Write a main idea sentence for the chapter you read today. If you didn't have a reading assignment, use a story you know well.

_____

_____

_____

Inferences

What can you infer from the following?

It's cold outside. I heard the song _Jingle Bells_ at the mall while I shopped for the perfect gift for my brother. Every house has decorative lights adorning the outside. There's a tree in my living room.

_____

I baked a dozen cookies last night. There are only two cookies left and I have a horrible stomach ache.

_____

Rex is my best friend. He wags his tail whenever he sees me. Rex loves to play fetch and has learned to sit, stay, roll over, beg, and shake. He loves it when I scratch his belly.

_____

Linking Verbs

Fill in the sentences below with the correct present tense linking verb from the box.

| am | is | are |

Your brother _____ fishing with his friends.

Katie and Stacey _____ eating lunch in the park.

My mom _____ feeling poorly today.

You _____ going to need a coat if you go outside.

I _____ tossing the football after dinner.

Fill in the sentences below with the correct past tense linking verb from the box.

| were | was |

We _____ running a marathon this past weekend.

His parents _____ renewing their vows last Saturday.

She _____ cheering loudly when her team won.

I _____ sailing on the lake when the storm came up.

You _____ singing so beautifully this morning.

Verbs

Not all past tense verbs end in –ed. In the blank, fill in the past tense form of the verb in parentheses.

The wind _____ hard all night long.
(to blow)

The airplane had _____ past the runway.
(to fly)

We all _____ running when we heard the crash.
(to come)

We _____ a candle in honor of our grandmother.
(to light)

The choir _____ beautifully this morning.
(to sing)

She _____ me home from the dentist.
(to bring)

I _____ an essay about Abraham Lincoln.
(to write)

My father _____ all the way to the finish line.
(to run)

She was _____ to the hospital in an ambulance.
(to drive)

Verbs

Choose the correct verb apple to fit on the tree.

Verbs and Adverbs

On the left blank of each row, write an action verb so that you have a list of ten when you have filled them all in. Then go back through and write an adverb beside each one that describes the verb you've written.

_____   _____

_____   _____

_____   _____

_____   _____

_____   _____

_____   _____

_____   _____

_____   _____

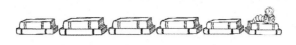

Writing

Write a story using your verbs and adverbs from lesson 147. Use at least half of them.

_____

_____

_____

_____

_____

_____

_____

_____

_____

_____

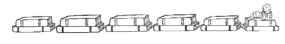

Grammar

Choose the correct word from the box to fill in the blank.

two	to	too

We are going _____ the concert tonight.

We have _____ extra tickets.

Maybe Grandma and Grandpa can come, _____ .

They like _____ go _____ bed early, though.

whose	who's

Do you know _____ jacket was left here?

Is it someone _____ going to be mad it's lost?

_____ going to make sure it's returned?

their	there	they're

We need to return them to _____ home.

It's across the street over _____ .

They might be in trouble if _____ late.

Verbs and Adverbs

Take your story from lesson 148 and try to replace each verb and adverb combo with a more specific verb. For example: *talk quietly* could be *whisper*; *walk quickly* could be *hustle*; *jump vigorously* could be *launch*. Write your verb/adverb combo and the new verb you're replacing them with on the lines below.

_____

_____

_____

_____

_____

Can you think of a more specific verb to replace these verb/adverb pairs? Write it on the blank beside each pair.

talk loudly   _____

sleep soundly   _____

fall down   _____

speak falsely   _____

breathe heavily   _____

Parts of Speech

Color the nouns blue, the verbs green, the pronouns yellow, the adjectives red, and the adverbs orange.

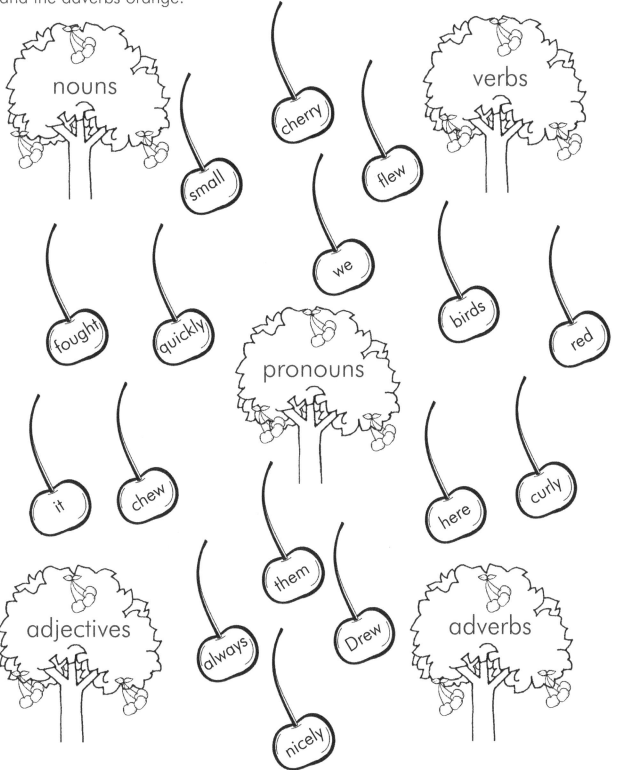

Vowel Sounds

Write the word from the box that has the same vowel sound as, but different spelling pattern from, the one given.

said	tweet	flop	loop
eye	sail	boat	from

jump _____   smile _____

nest _____   pane _____

blue _____   mow _____

seal _____   pawn _____

Adverbs

Underline the adverbs in the sentences below. There might be more than one. Do you know which words they are describing?

She hit her head on the very hard floor.

The sky was extremely blue after the terrifying storm.

Traffic is moving rather quickly today.

The view from the mountaintop was quite beautiful.

Noun Basketball

Color the common nouns blue and the proper nouns red.

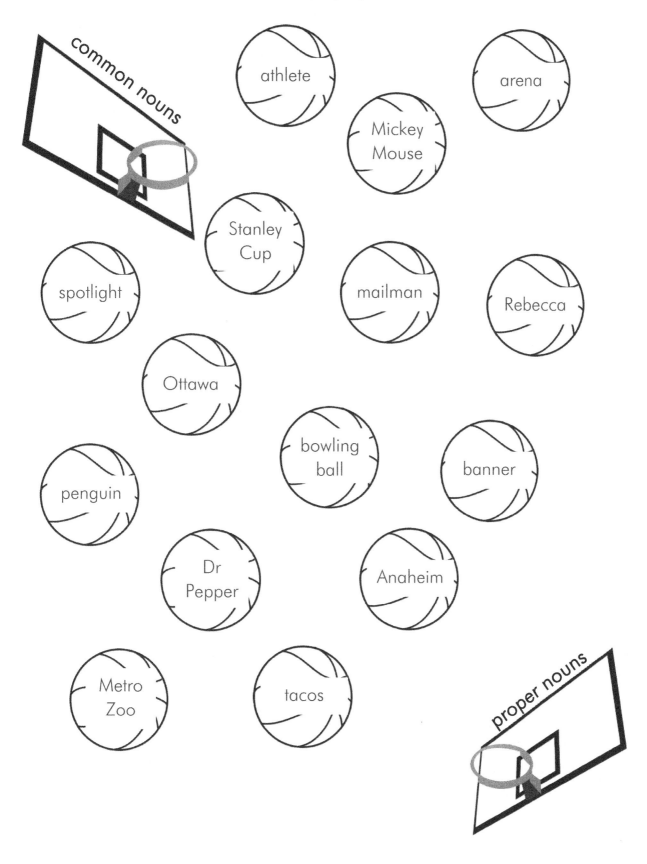

common nouns

athlete

arena

Mickey Mouse

Stanley Cup

spotlight

mailman

Rebecca

Ottawa

bowling ball

banner

penguin

Dr Pepper

Anaheim

Metro Zoo

tacos

proper nouns

Writing

Write a short story. To get started, go back to your reading from today and choose five words in a row. Use those five words all together in the same order in your story. Read your story to someone when you are done. Speak clearly and with inflection.

Spelling

Write your spelling words on the lines below as they are read to you from the Parent's Guide. Learn from any spelling mistakes you make.

_____   _____

_____   _____

_____   _____

_____   _____

_____   _____

_____   _____

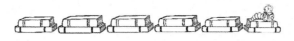

Correct the Sentences

For each sentence, choose the sentence type by circling it. Then underline any words that need to be capitalized, and add any punctuation.

show your work on your math paper.

       declarative   imperative   interrogative   exclamatory

Where can i find the spaghetti sauce

       declarative   imperative   interrogative   exclamatory

im so excited for my birthday!

       declarative   imperative   interrogative   exclamatory

i like to go to epcot at disney world in florida

       declarative   imperative   interrogative   exclamatory

Stop yelling at your sister

       declarative   imperative   interrogative   exclamatory

what is your favorite fruit

       declarative   imperative   interrogative   exclamatory

its a very cloudy day today

       declarative   imperative   interrogative   exclamatory

I cant believe how hot it is today!

       declarative   imperative   interrogative   exclamatory

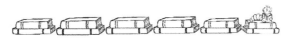

Homophones

Homophones are words that sound alike but have different spellings and/or meanings. For each sentence below, underline the homophone that best fits the sentence. Learn from any mistakes you make.

The ___ was eaten by the horse.	hay	hey
My backpack is ___.	knew	new
Rock climbing was quite the _____.	feet	feat
The bird _____ in the window.	flew	flu
My brother has _____ a lot this year.	groan	grown
I had to _____ the dough.	knead	need
It took us one _____ to get there.	our	hour

Homonyms

Homonyms are words that sound the same and have the same spelling but have different meanings. Read each sentence and fill in the homonym in the blank.

the opposite of dark or the opposite of heavy _____

the side of a river or a place full of money   _____

to have fun or a form of theater   _____

a tool with sharp teeth or past tense of see   _____

Writing

Write a short story using at least two sets of homonyms or homophones. Get a high five and a hug if you use three or more sets.

_____

_____

_____

_____

_____

_____

_____

_____

Friendly Letter

Do you remember how to write a friendly letter? Be sure to include the heading, salutation, body, closing, and signature.

_____

_____

_____

_____

_____

_____

_____

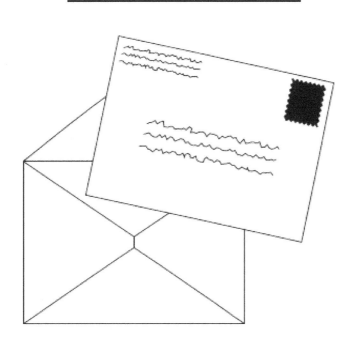

Acrostic Poem

Write an acrostic poem. Whatever the topic of your poem is, write it one letter at a time down the page. Then start each line with the letter of that line. For instance, an acrostic poem about the month of May might go like this:

Mother's Day
April showers brought flowers
Yearning for summer break

_____

_____

_____

_____

_____

_____

_____

_____

_____

Descriptive Writing

Describe a scene, a picture. Use this for your first sentence: *"The wind blew cold and dry."* What kind of setting do you imagine with that description? Just picture it and describe it. It's not a story. Nothing needs to happen. Just describe the picture you are imagining. What is there? What do you see, hear, smell, and feel? Write at least five sentences.

_____

_____

_____

_____

_____

_____

_____

_____

Descriptive Writing

Take your description from lesson 161. Add a character. Write a paragraph describing a character. It doesn't have to be a person. Put your character into the scene and describe your character. What does he look like and sound like? What is the character feeling being part of the scene you described? What is your character's name? How old is he? What is his favorite thing to do? You don't have to tell all of these things. Describe him so that we know all of these things. How can you describe him so that we can learn about him? Write at least five sentences.

_____

_____

_____

_____

_____

_____

_____

Descriptive Writing

Now write the next paragraph. Have something totally unexpected happen. How does it affect the character? How does it affect the scene? What does the character do in response?

_____

_____

_____

_____

_____

_____

_____

Descriptive Writing

Write the end of your story. What happens? Remember to be as descriptive as possible.

_____

_____

_____

_____

_____

_____

_____

_____

_____

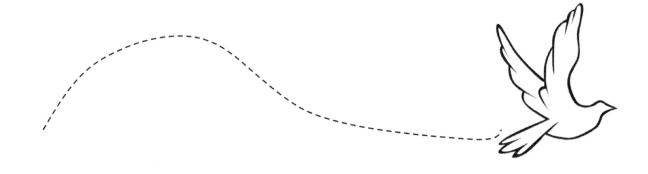

Editing Checklist

Read through your descriptive writing and fix any mistakes. Here is a modified editing checklist. Remember to aim for a check mark in each box.

First paragraph
☐ My first paragraph describes the picture I was imagining.
☐ My first paragraph includes at least five sentences.
☐ My first paragraph includes many descriptive words.

Second paragraph
☐ My second paragraph describes my character well.
☐ My second paragraph includes at least five sentences.
☐ My second paragraph includes many descriptive words.

Third paragraph
☐ My third paragraph has an exciting twist.
☐ My third paragraph tells how the character reacts to the twist.

Last paragraph
☐ My last paragraph ends the story well.
☐ My last paragraph has many descriptive words.

Unity
☐ My story flows well and makes sense.
☐ My story uses transition words.
☐ My story is interesting.

Subject Matter
☐ My story has different sentences – short, long, compound, complex.

Grammar/Mechanics
☐ All words are spelled correctly.
☐ There are no grammatical mistakes.
☐ There are no punctuation errors.
☐ There are no fragments.
☐ There are no run-on sentences.

Editing

Edit these sentences by underlining words that need to be capitalized and writing in any missing punctuation. Circle the words that are misspelled or misused. Do you know how to spell or use them properly?

sometimes when you got to the end of the year, its easy to get a little brain dead. its time for a scool break! You might be saying i dont want to have to think anymore. but its important to keep your brain focused and press on in your studys. Think about how much youve learned this year! You have written many different stories essays and main ideas. keep working hard in your writing. Maybe someday youll have a published book on the market. If so, i would love to have read it!

Final Project

Use this sheet to record your resources, or the places where you find information for your final project. The info lines are short on purpose. Don't try to copy a full sentence. Take notes like "made in 1902" or "born on July 6." This will help you not copy what others wrote. Record the website address and date you found the information or the name of the author and book title of a book you used.

Topic:_____

Resource 1:_____

Info:_____   Info:_____

Info:_____   Info:_____

Info:_____   Info:_____

Resource 2:_____

Info:_____   Info:_____

Info:_____   Info:_____

Info:_____   Info:_____

Resource 3:_____

Info:_____   Info:_____

Info:_____   Info:_____

Info:_____   Info:_____

Final Project

Continue to gather your research. Use this sheet to record your resources and notes for your project. Remember that the info lines are short on purpose. Just take notes instead of copying full sentences. This will ensure your work is your own and not copied from someone else.

Resource 4:_____

Info:_____   Info:_____

Info:_____   Info:_____

Info:_____   Info:_____

Resource 5:_____

Info:_____   Info:_____

Info:_____   Info:_____

Info:_____   Info:_____

Resource 6:_____

Info:_____   Info:_____

Info:_____   Info:_____

Info:_____   Info:_____

Final Project

This is your last day for researching and gathering facts. Look for any missing pieces you feel you have and jot your notes below.

Resource 7:_____

Info:_____   Info:_____

Info:_____   Info:_____

Info:_____   Info:_____

Resource 8:_____

Info:_____   Info:_____

Info:_____   Info:_____

Info:_____   Info:_____

Resource 9:_____

Info:_____   Info:_____

Info:_____   Info:_____

Info:_____   Info:_____

Final Project

Today, write your introduction. Remember that you want to make your opening line interesting to grab your reader's attention. Your introduction should make us want to read the rest of the paper. Also remember that your main idea should be the last line of your introduction.

_____

_____

_____

_____

_____

_____

_____

Final Project

Today you are going to organize. Think about your introduction. What is your thesis? What is the point you are going to make with your research report? You need to use your facts to make that point. Gather your facts into groups. All of the facts in each group should be about one part of your topic. Earlier in the year you had who/what, where/when, why/how groups. You can use those same groups again or choose different groups. Use the facts you have and see how they relate to each other. Color code them. Mark the ones that go together the same color. Then make a key. For instance, write "when" in blue and then draw a blue line through all of the when facts on your facts pages (or whatever groups you choose). Aim for five groups with at least 2 facts each. Write your key on the lines below.

_____

_____

_____

_____

_____

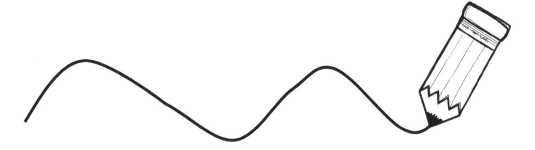

Final Project

Today you will continue organizing. Decide the order that you are going to use your groups. For instance, if you were doing the Panama Canal, you might have a paragraph of how it was designed, another about who worked on it and what the cost was, another about how it changed the world. All of these could even be split into more paragraphs depending on what facts you had to tell. Get all of your facts into groups. Label each group. Decide on their order and write it on this page.

_____

_____

_____

_____

_____

_____

_____

Final Project

Today you are going to take your topics and write an outline for the body of your report. Each capital letter should be a topic of a paragraph. Aim for *at least* five topics. Each lower case letter is a fact for that topic. If you have more than three facts for a topic, think about how you can divide the topic into two mini topics.

A. _____

    1. _____

    2. _____

    3. _____

    4. _____

B. _____

    1. _____

    2. _____

    3. _____

    4. _____

C. _____

    1. _____

    2. _____

    3. _____

    4. _____

(continued on next page)

D. _____

    1. _____

    2. _____

    3. _____

    4. _____

E. _____

    1. _____

    2. _____

    3. _____

    4. _____

F. _____

    1. _____

    2. _____

    3. _____

    4. _____

Final Project

Today start with your A and B topics on your outline from lesson 173 and begin writing. Remember that the first sentence of your paragraph gives the main idea for that paragraph. Each paragraph has a main idea sentence, details that tell about that idea, and a conclusion sentence. Use a mixture of short and long sentences that use words like and/because.

_____

_____

_____

_____

_____

_____

_____

_____

_____

Final Project

Write about topics C and D from lesson 173's outline following the correct format.
Be sure you are using transition words to get from one paragraph to the next.

_____

_____

_____

_____

_____

_____

_____

_____

_____

_____

Final Project

Write paragraphs for topics E and F from your outline if you have them. Continue to follow the proper format and use transition sentences.

_____

_____

_____

_____

_____

_____

_____

_____

_____

_____

Final Project

Write your conclusion. The first sentence of your conclusion retells your **thesis** or main idea of your report. Don't use the same exact sentence from your introduction. Reword your main idea. Then add another sentence and conclude with a final sentence. Your final sentence should give meaning to your report. Use the word "I" and tell what you think of the whole thing, why it is important.

_____

_____

_____

_____

_____

Editing Checklist

Read through your report and fix any mistakes. Here again is the list of things to keep track of as you edit. Aim for a check mark in each box.

Introduction
- ☐ My introduction begins with an attention grabber.
- ☐ My introduction has at least three sentences.
- ☐ My introduction ends with the main idea of my report.

Body
- ☐ The body of my report has at least three paragraphs.
- ☐ Each paragraph of the body starts with a topic sentence.
- ☐ Each paragraph of the body has at least three supporting sentences.
- ☐ Each paragraph of the body has a conclusion sentence.

Conclusion
- ☐ My conclusion has at least three sentences.
- ☐ My conclusion restates my main idea.
- ☐ My conclusion answers the question, "So what?"

Unity
- ☐ My report flows well and makes sense.
- ☐ My report uses transition words.
- ☐ My report is interesting.

Subject Matter
- ☐ My report has different sentences – short, long, compound, complex.
- ☐ My report uses descriptive words.
- ☐ All parts of my report support my main idea.

Grammar/Mechanics
- ☐ All words are spelled correctly.
- ☐ There are no grammatical mistakes.
- ☐ There are no punctuation errors.
- ☐ There are no fragments.
- ☐ There are no run-on sentences.

Final Project

Compile your bibliography using the guidelines in the Parent's Guide. Remember to list your sources alphabetically by author's last name. Start each resource on a new line. Write neatly and legibly.

_____

_____

_____

_____

_____

_____

_____

_____

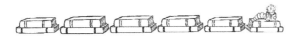

Final Project

Read your report to or with your family. Let them leave comments here about their favorite facts. Great job writing your research report!

I liked the report because: _____

_____

Something I learned was: _____

_____

I liked the report because: _____

_____

Something I learned was: _____

_____

I liked the report because: _____

_____

Something I learned was: _____

_____

(This page left intentionally blank)

The Autobiography of

_____

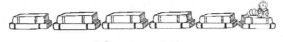

About Me

Fill in the following chart about yourself.

Name	Hobbies/Talents

Address	

	Interests

Parents' Names	

Siblings	Picture of me

Eye Color	Hair Color	

(continued on next page)

About My Mom

Fill in the following chart about your mom.

Name	Date of marriage

Date of birth	Place of marriage

Place of birth	Interests/hobbies/talents

Parents' Names

Siblings

Picture of my mom

Eye Color	Hair Color

(continued on next page)

About My Dad

Fill in the following chart about your dad.

Name	Date of marriage

Date of birth	Place of marriage

Place of birth	Interests/hobbies/talents

Parents' Names	

Siblings	Picture of my dad

Eye Color	Hair Color	

About My Brother

Fill in the following chart about your brother. If you have more than one brother you can print more pages from lesson 111 of LA 4 on our website.

Name	Any other information
Date of birth	
Place of birth	
Hobbies	
Interests	Picture of my brother
Eye Color / **Hair Color**	

(continued on next page)

About My Sister

Fill in the following chart about your sister. If you have more than one sister you can print more pages from lesson 111 of LA 4 on our website.

Name	Any other information
Date of birth	
Place of birth	
Hobbies	
Interests	Picture of my sister
Eye Color	Hair Color	

About My Grandmother - Paternal

Fill in the following pages about your grandparents. Ask your parents or call your grandparents (with permission!) if you need help with the information.

Name	Date of marriage

Date of birth	Place of marriage

Place of birth	Interests/hobbies/talents

Parents' Names	

Occupation	Picture of my grandmother

Date/place of death	

Eye Color	Hair Color	

(continued on next page)

About My Grandfather - Paternal

| Name | Date of marriage |

| Date of birth | Place of marriage |

| Place of birth | Interests/hobbies/talents |

| Parents' Names | |

| Occupation | Picture of my grandfather |

| Date/place of death | |

| Eye Color | Hair Color | |

(continued on next page)

About My Grandmother - Maternal

| Name | Date of marriage |

| Date of birth | Place of marriage |

| Place of birth | Interests/hobbies/talents |

| Parents' Names | |

| Occupation | Picture of my grandmother |

| Date/place of death | |

| Eye Color | Hair Color | |

(continued on next page)

About My Grandfather - Maternal

Name	Date of marriage

Date of birth	Place of marriage

Place of birth	Interests/hobbies/talents

Parents' Names	

Occupation	Picture of my grandfather

Date/place of death	

Eye Color	Hair Color

About My Great Grandmother – Paternal #1

Fill in the following pages about your great grandparents. Ask your parents or call your grandparents (with permission!) if you need help with the information.

Name	Date of marriage

Date of birth	Place of marriage

Place of birth	Interests/hobbies/talents

Parents' Names

Occupation

Picture of my great grandmother

Date/place of death

Eye Color	Hair Color

(continued on next page)

About My Great Grandmother – Paternal #2

| Name | Date of marriage |

| Date of birth | Place of marriage |

| Place of birth | Interests/hobbies/talents |

| Parents' Names | |

| Occupation | |

| Date/place of death | Picture of my great grandmother |

| Eye Color | Hair Color | |

(continued on next page)

About My Great Grandfather – Paternal #1

Name	Date of marriage
Date of birth	Place of marriage
Place of birth	Interests/hobbies/talents
Parents' Names	
Occupation	Picture of my great grandfather
Date/place of death	
Eye Color	Hair Color	

(continued on next page)

About My Great Grandfather – Paternal #2

Name	Date of marriage

Date of birth	Place of marriage

Place of birth	Interests/hobbies/talents

Parents' Names

Occupation

Picture of my great grandfather

Date/place of death

Eye Color	Hair Color

(continued on next page)

About My Great Grandmother – Maternal #1

| Name | Date of marriage |

| Date of birth | Place of marriage |

| Place of birth | Interests/hobbies/talents |

| Parents' Names | |

| Occupation | Picture of my great grandmother |

| Date/place of death | |

| Eye Color | Hair Color | |

(continued on next page)

About My Great Grandmother – Maternal #2

Name	Date of marriage

Date of birth	Place of marriage

Place of birth	Interests/hobbies/talents

Parents' Names

Occupation

Picture of my great grandmother

Date/place of death

Eye Color	Hair Color

(continued on next page)

About My Great Grandfather – Maternal #1

Name	Date of marriage

Date of birth	Place of marriage

Place of birth	Interests/hobbies/talents

Parents' Names	

Occupation	

Date/place of death	Picture of my great grandfather

Eye Color	Hair Color	

(continued on next page)

About My Great Grandfather – Maternal #2

Name	Date of marriage
Date of birth	Place of marriage
Place of birth	Interests/hobbies/talents
Parents' Names	
Occupation	Picture of my great grandfather
Date/place of death	

Eye Color	Hair Color

The Day I Was Born

Fill in this page about the day you were born. Ask your parents for any information you don't know.

Date of Birth

Time of Birth

Weight

Length

Place of birth

Doctor's Name

Any complications or memorable moments?

What was going on in the world the year I was born?

Picture of me as a baby

(continued on next page)

The Day I Was Born

Write the story of when you were born. What happened? How were your parents feeling? Who came to see you?

_____

_____

_____

_____

_____

_____

_____

_____

Special Things About Me

Fill in these boxes with the things that make you who you are. What are your talents and interests?

Words that describe me

Personality traits

Things I like to do

Picture of me doing something I love

(continued on next page)

Special Things About Me

Write the story of a special event in your life. Use lots of adjectives and adverbs to make it descriptive.

_____

_____

_____

_____

_____

_____

_____

_____

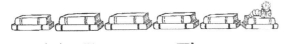

My Favorite Things

Fill in these boxes with the things that make you who you are. What are your talents and interests?

My Favorite Color	My Favorite Activities
My Favorite Book	
My Favorite Food	
My Favorite Song	
My Favorite Subject	Picture of me doing my favorite thing
My Favorite Movie	
My Favorite Animal	

(continued on next page)

My Favorite Things

Write a story of a special memory with one of your favorite things. Be as descriptive as you can.

_____

_____

_____

_____

_____

_____

_____

_____

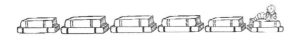

Places I've Lived

Fill in these boxes with information about the different places you've lived. You can draw a picture of your favorite place at the bottom.

Addresses or General Places I've Lived

Favorite Place I've Lived

Autobiography

Use this page to write the story of your life. You can use the other pages you've filled in about your family tree, your favorite things, special things about you, etc.

_____

_____

_____

_____

_____

_____

_____

_____

_____

_____

Congratulations!

You have finished Language Arts 4!

The Easy Peasy All-in-One Homeschool is a free, complete online homeschool curriculum. There are 180 days of ready-to-go assignments for every level and every subject. It's created for your children to work as independently as you want them to. Preschool through high school is available as well as courses ranging from English, math, science, and history to art, music, computer, thinking, physical education, and health. A daily Bible lesson is offered as well. The mission of Easy Peasy is to enable those to homeschool who otherwise thought they couldn't.

The Genesis Curriculum takes the Bible and turns it into lessons for your homeschool. Daily lessons include Bible reading, memory verse, spelling, handwriting, vocabulary, grammar, Biblical language, science, social studies, writing, and thinking through discussion questions.

The Genesis Curriculum uses a complete book of the Bible for one full year. The curriculum is being made using both Old and New Testament books. Find us online at genesiscurriculum.com to read about the latest developments in this expanding curriculum.

Made in United States
Orlando, FL
02 March 2023

30595216R00122